Get In The Flow
Destiny Is Calling

. . .

Get In The Flow
Destiny Is Calling

A Compilation
By Nell Dixon

ThrUs Publishing
Coppell Texas

• • •

Copyright

Printed in the United States of America.
First Printing, 2015

ISBN-13:978-09-864-0331-6

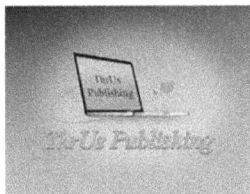

ThrUs Publishing
820 S. MacArthur Blvd #105-166
Coppell, Texas 75019

• • •

Dedication

I would like to dedicate this project to my awesome Teacher, Mentor, Life Coach, Friend and Husband Apostle C.D. Dixon. Apostle, thank you so much for believing in me, encouraging me when I really wanted to give up so many times and most of all thank you for pushing me to the finish line.

You are truly a Mighty 'Praying' Man of God. I am so sure that I truly contribute to those countless hours on your face calling on God. Nevertheless, your love has truly made it easy for me to flow into my *purpose* & *destiny*!

I would like to also dedicate this project to all the amazing 'Featured Authors' that believed in me and signed on to participate in this *dynamic* project to the Glory of God.

Thank you all for hearing the voice of God and partnering with me to push out *our* dreams!

• • •

"Commit your work to the Lord and your plans will be established."

Proverbs 16:3

• • •

Table of Contents

• • •

• • •

Acknowledgements

I would like to first thank the Lord for entrusting me with such a great mandate of birthing out this compilation book. I want to thank my wonderful Pastor, Friend, Spiritual Coach, Sweet breath of LIFE my awesome husband Apostle C.D. Dixon. Thank you for loving me *back to life*. Thank you for being my tailored-made answer from God! Thank you for birthing me out in prayer, training me in the prophetic and teaching me ministry protocol. Truly when the student was ready, the teacher showed up! You are an amazing teacher! Thank you from the bottom of my heart for *everything* that you have done and are doing for me!

I would like to acknowledge and appreciate our three wonderful children: Demarius, Taylor & Chesteria. Thank you for allowing us to love you all unconditionally. I would like to thank my parents for being a tremendous part of the birthing process for this project.

To all the *amazing* and anointed featured authors who trusted the God in me and heard the clarion call to join forces for this compilation project - Thank you so much. I appreciate all your

• • •

prayers, encouragement, participation and for making it easy for it to be a FLOW! Thank you all!

To the *amazing* Master Business Coach Tish Bell of Golden Business Success Mastery - My God Thank You! You have an amazing God-given gift to help the people propel their ministry and business to the next dimension. Thank you for all the information and practical principles that you shared with me to get me and this project UNSTUCK! You are truly called to the overdue – providing true results and not a bunch of meaningless hype. From the first day of coaching with you I experienced "IMMEDIATE" results. Thank you from the bottom of my heart.

Thank you all for *Getting In The Flow*!

~**Prophetess Nell Dixon**

Introduction

The *Get in the Flow: Destiny is Calling* compilation book was birthed out of a very pivotal time in my LIFE. *Get in the Flow* initially started out as a preaching & empowering tour. The goal was to help people, through the power of the Holy Ghost, to move out of complacency, to **seek** God and to **rise** up to their God Given purpose! The tour was designed to go into a number of different cities with the intent to empower, encourage and inspire the people in that city and region to **know** God.

While we were in Marshall, Texas at our Annual Holy Convocation, before each service I would assist my husband Apostle C.D. Dixon with intercessory prayer. That Thursday of the week long service the LORD began to tell me while sitting in our day session, "There is a sound that I'm listening for from Earth."

Then the Lord took me to the night service and I began to see the church praising God and shouting before the LORD. The Lord allowed me to hear the sound that He was listening for from us here on earth.

Once the day session service was over I immediately went to the Director of Music for the Convocation and told him what I had encountered from the LORD. I told him, "I am not a musician but I know the sound that the LORD is listening for." I asked him if he would go into prayer and inquire of the LORD to give him the sound that HE is wanting from us. Needless to say I was truly anticipating the service that night. I was standing in full expectation of what God was going to do.

It had already been a very challenging week for most of the delegates of the Convocation. Personally we were receiving so much spiritual warfare in the form of distractions and physical attacks in our bodies. But we understood that *destiny was calling* and we had to stay *in the flow* of what God was doing and wanted to do for His people!

Because we **sought** clarity, **rose** to the occasion and **knew** what our assignment was, we were able to press right pass every limitation! As the service proceeded, we hit the sound on Earth and the LORD immediately said to me, "The portal is open…there is a flow! There is a flow from Heaven for you down to Earth! *Get in the Flow – Destiny is calling!*"

~Prophetess Nell Dixon

Get In The Flow- The Call of Destiny!

Have you ever tried to *fit in* with what appeared to be the in-crowd? Did you always feel that there was something different about you no matter how you tried to conform to your surroundings? Was there always a feeling deep down in your spirit that kept screaming, "There has to be more to Life than this?" When destiny is calling there's always an undeniable fire in your heart that will NOT let you quit! It's a fire that was lit before you were ever conceived in your mother's belly - a fire of Purpose. The bible declares in **Jeremiah 1:5** "Before I formed you in the womb I knew you." We were all created for a God-given Purpose. Once you realize what that God-given Purpose is, that's when you really start moving toward fulfilling your Destiny!

I can remember so vividly as a young teenager having a desire to fit in with the people I thought were the "IN" crowd. You know the ones we make celebrities in our own minds. You know the popular peers that seem to have the *most* friends, the *latest* designer wears and the *coolest* cars. (We later mature into adulthood and realize all of those things are just superficial facets of a person's personality.) As I began to really flow through life I finally got to a place where I understood what MY purpose for being created was really for. Once I finally matured into and embraced the call on my life it seemed as though the whole host of HELL rose up against me. I didn't know this was all a part of Satan's plan to cause me to open my mouth and negatively speak against my own destiny. The bible clearly tells us in **Proverbs 18:21** "Death and life are in the power of the tongue." I knew that if I was going to fulfill my

God-given purpose successfully I had to
'*Get in the Flow*'.

As I began to pursue purpose I
found that my destiny was not just left
up to chance. I had to get divine
instructions from God on what to do,
how to do it and who to do it with. I
was so surprised to realize that as I
began to walk out this Master plan
called 'Life' step by step - life, as I knew
it, had totally changed forever. While
experiencing so many different things
according to God's mandate, I would
have to sometimes walk it out alone so it
seemed.

As my appetite grew more and
more for the things of God and less of
the flesh I immediately noticed my circle
of friends, family and colleagues began
to get smaller and smaller. Destiny was
calling and I had to condition myself to
be the ANSWER. I researched destiny, I
read books on destiny and I was so
intrigued. I wanted to know more about
this thing called Destiny. So I began to

pray and ask God to show me what my destiny and purpose was. I began to cry out on a regular basis in pursue of FIRE THAT WAS STILL DEEP IN MY HEART. "WHAT IS MY PURPOSE AND WHY WAS I CREATED?" I was trying to find my Flow. "Who am I? What is MY assignment for God's Glory? When was I going to get to the place where true 'FULFILLMENT' was achieved? Why does it seem so hard for me to flow in my destiny?" I had so many questions and LIFE began answering them one by one.

I remember the days and nights my husband and I cried out to God for Him to bless us with another baby. We were diligently working on our God given assignments: Pastoring, ministering to countless people, raising our family and pursuing our Purpose as we knew it to be. During that time I had been having several dreams about my great grandmother dying and every time I would have one of those dreams I would immediately wake up and intercede for her. No matter what the situation was God would always answer and she would make it through. I can recall this one night so vividly that in my dream I saw her. She was dressed up for church. She had a beautiful gold jewel necklace around her neck and she was carrying a present in her hand. She was trying to cross the street and I remember in the dream opening my mouth to say, "*Ma 'ma* where are you going?" However in the natural as I opened my mouth to call her name I began to choke and woke up in a panic.

Now anyone that knows me knows that my grandmother (my great grandmother's daughter) was my absolute heart. When my grandmother, *Mary,* passed away many years ago, I deemed my great grandmother, *Ma 'ma,* as the only tangible thing in this earth realm that I had left to connect me to my grandmother. So I wasn't so quick to want to let that go. I did not realize that her destiny had been fulfilled here on earth and she was trying to be released from this realm as we know it. Finally, that day came and I sat in the services and cried for 2 ½ hours straight grieving for life fulfilled not knowing God had answered my husband and I prayer for another baby. Yes, we were finally pregnant again. Eight days after finding out that we were expecting we began to lose the baby - talk about destiny and purpose being revealed all at the same time. The very day I was being taken into emergency surgery while miscarrying the promise, was also our oldest daughter's high school graduation. After experiencing a series of heart heavy ordeals with losing the baby I was left wondering what is the Purpose of all of this. Surely, God wasn't getting the Glory out of this.

As I lay in bed recovering from emergency surgery I began to pray and cry out to the Lord, "How can this be?" Not understanding that even in the midst of the pain, God was still stretching me for Purpose. Days passed and I didn't want to get out of bed, have no company nor talk to anyone about anything. Yes, depression was setting in. During one early morning cry I heard the Lord say, "Have a Prayer Clinic." I immediately got offended. I was whining and telling God, "I'm grieving. Why can't someone pick me up in the spirit and pray for us?" I didn't understand that Destiny was calling and I had a mandate to fulfill for God's purpose - grieving or not. Regardless of my grief, destiny had to be fulfilled. I made the clarion call and gathered the saints together for the Prayer Clinic in two weeks. Boy did God get the glory out of that service. Five months later we were pregnant again and delivered a beautiful baby girl that loves the LORD!!

As I reflect back on the many test and trials (even after that incident), I understood that when you are pursuing Destiny and flowing in your God-given purpose you can't allow any distractions to distort your vision or shift your focus off the mission at hand. No matter what form the distraction presents itself in, it is imperative to stay connected to the plan of God for *your* life.

No one can stop *your* flow but *you*. No one has the power to divert *your* Destiny from being fulfilled but *you*. God has a purpose and a plan for *your* life.

Get in the Flow: Destiny Is Calling!
~Prophetess Nell Dixon

PROPHETESS *Nell Dixon* has
been empowered with an immaculate
three-fold Prophetic, Evangelistic and
Pastoral anointing to deliver the Word
of God. Prophetess ministers with such
a boldness that it causes even the
hardest of hearts to be pierced by the
love of God. Prophetess Nell Dixon is
known as a woman after the heartbeat
of God. This is very evident by a
lifestyle of prayer, fasting and holiness
that she leads diligently before the Lord.

Prophetess Dixon has been
commissioned to share the good news of
Jesus Christ to the nations of the world.
She is a devoted wife to Apostle C.D.
Dixon and mother to three beautiful
children. Prophetess is an honor
graduate of Hargest Business College,
graduating Magna Cum Laude in
Accounting. With a social awareness of
the economic issues of today's time,
Prophetess Nell is also an entrepreneur.

Prophetess Dixon serves as a
licensed and ordained Executive Pastor

of Spiritual Temple World Headquarters where her husband, Apostle C.D. Dixon, is both Senior Pastor and Overseer. Also, serving as the Executive Assistant to Apostle Dixon, Prophetess and Apostle Dixon are the proprietors of many conferences and events including but not limited to: *From Chains-2-Freedom, The Refreshing Wind Prayer Clinic, Prophetic Wind Radio Weekly Broadcast, Get In The Flow Tour, Couples with a Love Affair, Empowering the Business Mind, Prophetic Youth Explosion, Prophetic Night Live and The Gift that Heals.*

As Prophetess Dixon is currently working on her compilation book, *Get In The Flow,* she is envisioned with the mandate to point those that are lost back to JESUS, help the hurting and empower those who really want change in their lives for the better.

Prophetess Nell Dixon is fully equipped to take the message of Christ to the world.

Prophetess Nell Dixon

Facebook *
www.facebook.com/ProphetessNellDixon

Twitter *
www.twitter.com/ProphetessNellD

Instagram *
www.Instagram.com/ProphetessNellDixon

Email *
NellDixonMinistries@hotmail.com

"But **seek** *ye first the kingdom of God,"*

Matthew 6:33

Seek God– The Anointing

Thursday, June twenty-fifth two thousand fourteen, while in service I asked God to give me a special anointing. Not just a regular anointing that anyone can have but rather a biblical anointing that He gave his leaders in the bible. For instance:

- Prophet Isaiah could see beyond and after his time
- Apostle Paul was able to win many souls to Christ
- Apostle Peter's shadow could heal the sick

In response to this petition, God put me on a sanctification and consecration fast. God told me to take three days out of the next three months to fast, so I did. Friday morning I woke up around six in the morning which is hard and unusual for me because I'm not a morning person. I know, "The early bird catches the worm," but I enjoy my sleep. I woke up and fell back to sleep praying. I did this four times before finally getting up all the way. Once I was fully awake, I did something that's hard for most teenagers to do - I signed out of all my social media apps in my phone, didn't answer phone calls and purposely ignored text messages. Even though my brothers wanted to hangout, I instead went to my garage and stayed in there all day until six o'clock that evening. While in there I made me a place to study and pray using a cover and some boxes left over from moving into our new home. I did something most people wouldn't do but I also asked for something most people wouldn't ask for. I was once told by a wise young lady, "In order for you to get something special from God you have to have a special relationship with God." So, in order to have a special relationship you have to do something special or hold a special place in His heart. You wouldn't treat your child the same way you treat your co-worker would you? No, why not? Because, although your co-worker and yourself do have a relationship, it is not the same type of relationship that a parent has with their child. So, of course a child can get something from their parent that a co-worker cannot because of the different dimensions of their relationship. That's why if I asked the Father to give me something as a son, I have to have a Father and son relationship - not just a religion. I sincerely asked God to give me something that was bigger and greater than me. I wanted a real anointing. I told God when I began ministry, "If you called me to it, then you have to anoint me for it." I never wanted to be a 'Modern day preacher.'

Yes, I'm liable to fall. No I'm not perfect but I didn't want to have the ability to preach well but have horrible character. I didn't want to be able to pull down power from heaven or be anointed in the pulpit but live an unholy lifestyle outside the church. I never wanted to become comfortable in my struggle with sin. One of the worst things we can ever do is become so comfortable with our struggle that we don't realize that we're bound. The sad part is that a lot of people will use the scripture to justify their struggle and believe that it's right. Since when did it become OK for Christians to twist the scripture around to justify their wrong? Since when did it become OK for us to sin and minister yet live without conviction? If we lose our conviction we'll also lose our standards, our morals and soon after, our connection or relationship with God. If we lose our standards for God and His house (The Church) we'll also begin to lose the importance of being connected to God. What good is it if we are only connected to the supplies but not connected to the source of the supplies? Wouldn't that make us the same as a 'gold-digger?'

There's only so much that I can expect from somebody that I don't have a connection with. I can't ask God to give me a special kind of anointing if I don't have a connection with him. You would look at a stranger crazy if he asked you for something that is very precious to you. You wouldn't give anybody anything that's very precious and valuable to you if there's no level of trust between you two. How do you know that you can trust a person with something valuable to you? There has to be a way that proves that the trust between the two is real and pure, such as a test or even time. With God, many times when we ask Him for something, He'll make us wait to test our faith. It is impossible to truly trust a person without having faith in that person. Sometimes God will even make you give something up in order for you to get what He has for you. You can't receive anything else if your hand, mind, spirit or heart is already full. God has a proven track record that what He gives you is far better than what He tells you to give up. After seeing what all comes with obtaining such a gift, the questions become: How bad do you really want it? How important is it to have what you asked God for? Are you willing to give something up for it? Are you willing to do what it takes to get it? What are you going to do with it? And lastly, Why do you want it? Is it for selfish gain or is it for the perfecting of the saints? Is it to obtain fame and fortune or to glorify God and exalt his name? Is It to feel fulfilled by feeding off the respect and applauds of people or because you really love God?

It's always a bad day to go after the right thing with the wrong intentions. What good is it if I have a great anointing but I don't use it for the right reason or the right way? What kind of person am I if the gift that God has given me to bless His people with, I use it for self-gain?

A man made fulfillment is merely a momentary high, but a God-made fulfillment is a lifetime of success. The dangerous part is that we ask God for blessings that we're not prepared to maintain. There's nothing worse than finally getting what God has promised you but shortly losing it because you weren't prepared to keep it. Don't ask God for anything that you're not willing to go after or ready to keep. The anointing of God is holy, sacred and pure. It is not supposed to be tainted, used wrongfully or contaminated. To obtain such a gift from God we have to live up to the standard that is required of us. **Luke 12:48 KJV** "...For unto whomsoever much is given, of him shall much be required..."

~Minister Joshua Campbell

MINISTER *Joshua Campbell* was born to Bishop Terrence & Lady Sharonda Campbell, May Ninth Nineteen Ninety Seven. He was born and raised in Marshall, Texas and moved to Dallas, Texas at the age of seventeen where he now resides with his mother, stepfather and four brothers.

Joshua Campbell is a fourth generation preacher. He began preaching at the age of eleven and became a licensed Minister at the age of twelve at his grandfather's church where he still faithfully attends. He began evangelizing at the age of thirteen.

At the age of sixteen he began his own international youth outreach ministry named *Kan You Move* Ministries. *Kan You Move* Ministries (KYM) has been growing in grace since the launching of the ministry. In the first year, over one hundred-forty members around the world joined this new fellowship. He is known to be a preacher, prophet, teacher, mentor, big brother and now an author.

Minister Campbell has a strong burning passion for helping people and seeing Gods people blessed. "God has given me the duty and vision to save the lost and strengthen the saved." Joshua says. His reason for doing what he does is not for fame or fortune, but to show light in someone else's dark tunnel. He wants people to look at him and be inspired to pursue their dreams and their God designed destiny.

He is currently finishing his first official book called *#IAmADreamer* and trying to make any positive effect on the world that he can.

Minister Joshua Campbell

Facebook * Joshua Campbell

Instagram * JC_Productions

Email *
kanyoumoveministries@gmail.com

Website *
www.Kanyoumoveministries.weebly.com

Seek Wisdom - Be the Light

Boom Blitz Poof and in the blink
of an eye my life was transformed when
I made the choice to accept what I have
always felt deep within myself. Finally I
stopped running, I stopped panicking
and I stopped feeling incomplete. When
I accepted Jesus into my life
wholeheartedly, it changed me and I
have never been the same. I had to step
back and really question myself, "What
was the real reason I wouldn't give
myself to God completely? What was
holding me back? Was it fear? Was it
doubt? Was it because I was more
concerned about what everyone else
would think if I became this bold, Holy
Ghost filled, powerful woman in God?"
Well if I can just be transparent, for me
it was "D", all of the above. I was
fearful. I had doubts. I didn't fully grasp

that I would be even greater than I could imagine by connecting with God. Everything that I experienced outside the will of God was nothing compared to what He really wanted to do in my life.

So my question for you is, "Have you ever been so secure in a choice you made that no matter what anyone else had to say about it you could relax and be comforted in the fact that you made the absolute best decision?" Well I will let you in on a little secret, when you step into the fullness of God's Kingdom that will be the exact feeling you will experience. Out of all the things we as people can do, be, wish or have - hands down being blood bought and saved by Jesus Christ is a no brainer. Let us pause and think about this for a minute. Did you know that you have already WON? No really, you are on the winning team in everything you do - no matter what the devil tries to present to you. God knows all, He has all and He wants to see his children experience ALL he has to offer. Now I don't know about anyone else, but it would only be foolish to be connected to anything else otherwise.

I finally realized why the devil would fight me so hard, try to distract me and get me out of my destined place. It was because he knew better than anyone that once I connected to God, kill my flesh and surrender my will I became one of Gods powerful children.

Whatever I could think of, whatever I desired, whatever I wanted to come into my life was in the palm of my hands. God has a purpose and plan for every single one of us. We were not birthed into this world by accident. God has a plan for us even when we don't exactly know what it is. God made no mistake by creating you - He knew exactly who you would become. The devil thinks that by putting obstacles in your way and trying to take your focus off of God that he WON. God is real.

God loves us. God has divine purpose for us. It's our job however to stay connected to that purpose, to the real reason we are here on this earth.

Let us pause and think what obstacles have been put in your way to get your focus off of God and the purpose of your life? Has it been a relationship? Has it been social media? Has it been your flesh? God wants to renew our minds and transform us into His magnificent image and all the devil thinks he has to do is put a thought into your mind that turns into actions.

I'm here to tell you that no matter what type of temptation or obstacle the devil brings to you, you CAN OVERCOME anything with the help of God. God is our father, He is our friend and He is our protector, our shoulder to cry on and our counselor. So don't think of God as some far away being - He is with us always. All we have to do is talk to Him, communicate, be completely transparent before Him and genuinely ask for His help. God will see about us every single time!

That's why I REFUSE to accept what the devil tries to present to me and you should too. It's time, as young adults in God, for us to take our rightful place in the Kingdom of God. We are Kings and Queens of the almighty so lack, unhappiness, depression, complacency, doubt, low self-esteem and anything else that's not focusing us back to the real MVP needs to be shaken off and snapped out of. God destined us to be great, to be leaders, to be the fire that ignites the power of God in every place we step into.

SO STOP and REALIZE IT'S OUR TIME. It's time to stop accepting and allowing what we see in this world to disconnect us from our destiny and inheritance with our Father. It's time to start challenging ourselves to be the example for which our generation follows. No more following, it's time to LEAD. Get from within the crowds, push your way to the front and point God's people back towards Him. We must not forget that this is not our home. This is not our ending place. Greater is ahead for us but we must stay connected, focused and begin to tune out anything that would pull us away from our real purpose.

So I encourage you, leaders of God, that regardless of what is placed in our view we will have the victory every time. This is not the time to be weak-minded. God has given us all the power we need to get through the obstacles the devil may try to bring to us. REALIZE that our time is NOW. The REVOLUTION is here. We are going to build the Kingdom of God with our passion, our commitment and faithfulness through the Love of God. We are royalty, we have been set apart. Make a BOLD stand for God and waiver not. We are the VICTORS in everything we do with Christ on our side. I speak into your life as a BOLD LEADER, A

WOMAN OF GOD and A
TRAILBLAZER: BE ENCOURAGED, BE
STRONG and KNOW THAT GOD
WILL NEVER LEAVE YOU NOR
FORSAKE YOU. TRUST AND BELIEVE
IN THE LORD WITH YOUR WHOLE
HEART AND HE WILL GIVE YOU
ALL THE STRENGTH YOU NEED TO
BE THE FIRE THAT IGNITES THE
PATH FOR MORE LEADERS TO TAKE
THEIR RIGHTFUL PLACE.

~Taylor Fisher

Be the Light Challenge

I'm calling out all the leaders: people who know God destined them for greatness, radical believers, people who know God has always been and will always be the answer and real warriors for Christ to step up and stand with me to be the light for our generation. Let the light of God shine through you, your lifestyle, your language and your appearance. Let's be the example that's putting the focus back to the real reason of our existences which is to glorify God in all things. Trust me when I say, give yourself to the Lord wholeheartedly and watch - **BOOM BLITZ POOF** you are transformed!

SISTER *Taylor Fisher* is excited about impacting her generation for JESUS!!! One of her main goals in life is to encourage, uplift and inspire her generation. "We must be Bold for GOD, share the good news about the KINGDOM OF GOD & exemplify the LOVE OF GOD to a generation that needs it the most!" says Fisher.

Taylor discovered her passion while writing the weekly news article for her church *Houston Spiritual Temple* where she was the Youth Director. What she would like everyone who reads her literary piece to know is that no matter your age, race or political views, we are all a part of God's Kingdom and we all have a part to play as we step into the fullness of God.

Fisher exclaims, "My generation will continue to be a catalyst to point people back to the only reason we were initially put on this earth. This is to be a true representation of Jesus Christ."

Taylor Fisher

Email * TaylorFisher18@gmail.com

Seek Sanctity–
The Price I Had To Pay
To Stand For Holiness

NO DISCOUNTS HERE! Have you ever seen a beautiful dress in a store that you got really excited about? The fabric and color was so perfect that you decided to purchase it. However, you were struck with mere disappointment when you looked at the price tag. The item you desired was extremely expensive and it appeared to be more than you could afford. When you realized how costly it was, you were taken aback by the price. At this point, you would resolve to put the dress back or say that you would come back at a later date when you could afford it.

Many of us have experienced a price beyond which we can imagine to pay. We often look later for the item to go on sale or to be discounted.

However, I have learned a valuable lesson! In life, quality things are costly.

This is how it is with holiness which seems to be a taboo topic. In this day and age, many people don't want to be associated with the word holiness because of what it cost and the stigma associated with it. Holiness requires much from a person and there are no discounts to achieve it. In the eyesight of God, He's calling for quality over quantity.

When we look at holiness in the natural, we can equate this scenario with gaining a high quantity of unnecessary things. However in the Spirit, God is calling for a higher quality, not something that can be purchased because He has already paid the price for us to stand in holiness with Him. One and one doesn't add up to be two.

Now that we understand that there are no shortcuts. Let me take a moment and define what holiness is. Holiness, according to Webster, is a state or quality of being holy; sanctified, Godliness, blessedness and piety. I personally define holiness as clean living, one who is striving to be Christ-like. In other words, there is a portrayal of Christ in all of your endeavors and interactions. The holiness of God is understanding the power of God at work in humanity. Holiness is not something you can earn but rather something that is given to you when you are submitted to God.

There are many people conveying a message that holiness is an equation that makes sense. I find this debatable because the transformation to holiness doesn't always add up. God is the only one that takes nothing and creates something. The state of being holy (like Christ) is not about a list of "I can't do this or I can't do that", but more so about a God who can do anything! Often times when I was younger, I used to sit and watch as the people would preach the word of God and I used to tell myself, one day that was going to be me. We may not have a clue as to what is going on in our lives, however, the God I serve knows best and he knows all. I never imagined that years later God would be using me as a vessel and allowing me to experience the feeling which I would describe as 'one of the best I've ever felt' in saving souls and witnessing a person dedicate their life to Christ.

There are so many people out there who were told holiness was about not being able to wear makeup, not wearing pants and jewelry, or attend games or movies. You just simply couldn't have fun anymore. This is certainly not true. The bible tells us in **2 Corinthians 3:17** that, "…where the spirit of the lord is there is liberty." When you serve the Lord you are given a liberty which is not given as an occasion to sin but it's given to enjoy the gift of life.

Jesus paid it all.

As a young child, I knew that the Lord always had a call on my life because I was a dreamer. In addition to this, God gave me a prophetic gift. I could hear people say negative things about me before I walked in a room. I would know things before they happened and I thought I was strange. I wanted to be used by God but here I am leading a difficult life.

I got pregnant at the tender age of 16 years old and had a baby at 17. I got married at 18 and I was still a baby myself. Needless to say the marriage didn't last but the best thing that came out of it was my son whom I love with all of my heart. I went through so many changes: abandonment, abuse, loneliness and rejection. But I always remembered to pray. It was during this time that I met Christ and made a decision that no matter what my devastation turned out to be, that I would serve the Lord by living holy.

Living a life of holiness has cost me everything. My life changed but I knew that I must stick with the decision, keep an open relationship with Christ and maintain my integrity, while fasting, praying and reading the word of God. I suffered many things and here I was a broken young lady, seemingly all alone. One would think that all of my family would be happy about my salvation, but sadly some of them would say I was losing my mind. I found out that you will have to give up some things for the cause of Christ which sometimes seems like a loss but in actuality, they are a gain. **Luke 18:29-30** says, "Yes, Jesus replied, "and I assure you that everyone who has given up house or wife or brothers or parents or children, for the sake of the kingdom of God, will be repaid many times over in this life and will have eternal life in the world to come." I found someone that I could really lean, trust and depend on and his name was Jesus.

When I began to totally embrace all that Jesus had for me, I became a preacher of the gospel. He blessed me with a man of God that loves me to life and I am now able to minister to people, pulling them out of the pit that I was once in. It is a rewarding and humbling experience to say the least.

God knew I had a work to do, so he gave me a man of God who feels the same way as I do. When you have someone in your corner who understands your position in life and you are both working towards a common goal, God will always show up to bless your hands to complete his promise. A lot of time people see what they perceive as the glory however, they don't know the story. If I had not surrendered one hundred percent to do the will of God, I would not be who I am today. I am a living example that if you trust God, lean on him, read the word and depend totally on him, God will always bring you out victoriously.

The price of holiness started with a decision. It started with learning to trust God through every decision and stand still through the process until I got to my promise. Through all of what I have gone through, I didn't charge God foolish. Some people mistakenly believe, that once you accept Jesus in your life, that life becomes a smooth road. Even though I was new to living a life for Christ and at times things were not easy, I didn't realize that these things had to happen to bring forth the complete transformation I was undergoing. God was teaching me just how I needed to be totally dependent upon him. God had great plans for me and he knew exactly who the woman of God I was destined to be. That's why I've been tried and tested from out of my mother's womb.

I remember the struggles I had to go through just to get back and forth to the house of God. I remember wanting to go to church and not having transportation, wanting to pay my tithes and not have a dime; wanting to look nice and having only one dress. It was at that moment God placed a special lady in my life by the name of Shirley. She helped me get to church. She even shared her money with me often times when she didn't even have much. When times became unbearable, I would always find myself saying, "Let go and let God." I am who I am today because I put all my faith in God and allowed him to take control over my life. The God in me truly preserved my life. It would be easy to become a failure. It would be easy to become all the negative things that people spoke over my life, but when you truly have God living on the inside of you, His will is what's best.

When you feel you can't carry on, call on God. When you feel like the world is against you, call on God. When you don't know how you will make it, call on God. Just remember when your back is against the wall, call on God.

And when He answers, you too will be able to tell the story of the price you had to pay for holiness! God bless you!

~Apostle Annie S Hinnant

APOSTLE *Annie S. Hinnant* was born January 16, 1954 in Clayton, North Carolina to the late Boston and Elizabeth Peacock Sanders. She is the youngest of ten siblings and it was obvious from birth that she was a different child. Anointed from birth and chosen for such a time as this, Apostle Annie Hinnant gained strength and courage from her Mother's advice to be strong and not to break under the pressures of life.

Apostle Annie Hinnant attended public school in Clayton, NC and graduated from Johnston Technical Community College in April 1972. She attended Shaw University in Raleigh, North Carolina receiving a Bachelor's Degree in Behavioral Science with concentrations in Psychology and Sociology. She has received her Master's Degree in Christian Education and Divinity.

Apostle Hinnant also has an Honorary Doctorate Degree with

Abundant Life Bible College and Theological Seminary. Understanding the importance of continuing education, Apostle Hinnant is furthering her education with Apex School of Theology, in receiving her Doctorate in Divinity.

Apostle Annie Hinnant is married to Chief Apostle Allan Hinnant, her soul mate and the love of her life. She has one son, a lovely daughter in-law, three grandsons and one great grandson. Their blessed union is a role model for married couples that have been graced by their presence. They founded the *Power of Praise Tabernacle of Deliverance* in Benson, NC in 1997. She stands with him under their organization of *Kingdom Connection Fellowship of Churches*, where five churches are directed under their leadership. There have been many sons and daughters that have been birthed through this ministry. Apostles, Prophets, Pastors, Teachers and

Evangelists are now walking and working in this five-fold ministry.

Apostle Annie Hinnant is the founder of *Annie S. Hinnant Ministries*, where *God's Woman by Design* has been established. Women from all walks of life join together meeting quarterly throughout the year for empowerment and refreshing. She has also established *D.I.V.A's*, which stands for *Divinely Inspirational Virtuous and Anointed Women of God*, ranging from 20-40 years of age. Annie S. Hinnant Ministries teaches women how to honor God through a virtuous life as stated in the Word of God.

Apostle Annie Hinnant is known as a Resuscitator in the Spirit. She always says that the fear of not obeying God is greater than the fear of satan coming after you for obeying. One of her favorite sayings is: His Favor, His Presence, His Power, His Glory and Our Victory. And we say today, "To God Be The Glory For The VICTORY!"

Apostle Annie S. Hinnant

Telephone * 919-413-8099

Instagram * Annie_Hinnant

E-Mail * Pastorhinnant@Aol.Com

Website * Annieshinnantministries.Org

Seek Freedom – Move Forward in Your Flow

You possess the power to move forward. It's already in you whether you know it or not. You are never too anointed, famous, or intellectually inclined that your self-check examinations have little use. There must be a constant and continuous surrender of your will, emotions, thoughts and desires. Grab hold to the spirit of God and the perfect law of liberty **James 1:25**, the law of love **1Cor.13:1-13; Ephes. 3:19**and dismiss all that oppose it. Dress yourself daily in the full armor of God **Ephes. 6:10-18**, the armor of light **Rom.13:12**, put on the Lord Jesus **Rom. 13:14**and proceed in the direction where the Spirit of God leads you. *"For as many as are led by the Spirit of God, these are the sons of God."* **Rom. 8:15**

You have the power to break free, stay free and live free. You have to want to be in peace more than you want to prove points and prove that you are right. You can choose to not give in to the thoughts, influence and strongholds of hurt, pain, shame and disappointment as well as anger, resentment, bitterness and un-forgiveness. These are toxic to you, your health and the active life of victory in the believer. I have been right there and had to choose to Move!

I couldn't allow myself to continue in the role of the victim when Christ has already given me the Victory. As a little girl, I could see in my environment and immediate life all of the things that I *didn't* want in the life of my future children, so I began to seek for ways to change that. I found my answers in having a personal relationship with Jesus Christ because all the wrong things were very real in the lives of the church but I didn't believe that had to be the end result for me.

No Religion! Move! Move from tradition to relationship and trust Him, the Lord, more than you trust anyone or anything. Move your mind to be able to move forward. Move!

Let me tell you something, praying others free and being in bondage yourself is a mixture for self-destruction. Knowing Jesus and the love of God for everyone else but having a constant emptiness and void in your own life is a life of hidden mystery and you will soon self-destruct. Confront what secretly confronts and tries to defeat you. Unblock your flow to yourself by freeing yourself!

In the bible there was a young boy that was often times thrown in the fire and the water. His father took him to the disciples who could not heal him. So Jesus asked the boy's father, "How long has he been like this?" Jesus addressed what many of us won't - when did it all begin! The father had a role to play in this as well. He needed to know that this could have been fixed a long time ago if he had identified the issue and believed.

Many of the readers of this book have been silenced a long time and it started in their childhood. The issues people have as adults most likely started from some childhood gate left open through issues, habits, events, accidents, trauma, suppression, depression, oppression, neglect, rejection, abuse or a slew of other damaging occurrences that were never addressed. Unfortunately, as adults there are struggles mentally, emotionally, spiritually, physically and financially. Let's move! Move towards your recovery, healing and deliverance. Deliverance is the children's bread. Take a seat and eat from the table of the Lord.

You or someone you know needs to know how to flow and move unhindered, delivered and free from the monster called 'THE PAST'. Pray on purpose. Fast on purpose. Speak the word of God on purpose. Take control of your soul, heart, mind and body again on purpose for purpose. How? By not believing the lies of your past and the devil any longer. You are not what you did. Stop agreeing with emotions that end destructively like anger, envy, and jealousy, feelings of hurt, bitterness and lack. It's time to live *better* and not *bitter*!

Never assume that you don't need deliverance, repentance or to forgive. If you practice freedom in yourself, you can effortlessly and effectively minister that to others with divine results of liberty and great joy.

When we fear God with Godly fear and reverence, we will constantly repent, renounce, forgive, release and seek to live at peace with ourselves and others. That's what love does. Love does not spread toxic information and experiences to beguile others or to exalt one's own self. The bible says love is kind and keeps no record of wrongs. So let us remember that when we become self-employed jailers of people locked in the stony places of the prisons of our hearts. Let us not disregard the grace of God and the freewill to forgive.

We really do have this ministry called reconciliation. Let us use it to break the chains, unsuccessful cycles and repeat offenses of our lives and others. Take control of what has once controlled and ruled you. Be accountable of all of your short comings and strive towards the mark of your high calling which is in Christ Jesus. Unblock your flow! I did. I did it by everything that I am telling you and then some. I will also tell you to love yourself, believe in you, bring deliverance to you and surrender you to the Lord in every area of your life without making excuses to stay the same or to blame someone else. Remember you are not a victim but you are and can continually be victorious. Live like you know it!

Your best days are still yet ahead of you and your worst days are behind you. Launch out into the deep and shun the shallow places of hopelessness. Get out of the boats of pity, procrastination, accusation, victimization and walk on those waters of life by faith. Yes, the winds will blow, (circumstances will come to distract you) the waves will rage, (discouragements, fears, doubts, unbelief) but you can stay focused by keeping your eyes on Jesus, your desires on Jesus and your mind on Jesus. He left His peace for you and I - receive it!

You might need to pray the prayer that I and many others have, will and still do pray, "Lord, I believe but help my unbelief," and "Lord, deliver me from me so that I can be delivered from people". Don't let pride trick you out of your best place. Pride is cruel and binds you to the blockages of your own flow. Defeat pride by humbling yourself to the Lord. Pursue peace. God will fight for you and through you accordingly.

You must apply the power of **Romans 8:28** "And you know that all things work together for the good...". Yes, it works for the good but you have to *know* it. When you know it, you *own* it! In spite of the unpleasant process, the working of the good is the mystery hidden in plain sight after the 'know' is established. Knowing is believing.

Believing positions you for the receiving. Hold your position of faith and grow in the grace given. The story is not over yet. Your life is just beginning. "For I am persuaded that neither death nor life, nor angels, nor principalities, nor powers, not things present nor things to come, **^39** nor height nor depth, nor any other created thing, shall be able to separate us from the love of God, which is in Christ Jesus our Lord." **Rom. 8:38-39.** But I want to leave you even more empowering words to live by, "Yet in all things, you are more than a conqueror through Him who loved you." **v.37**

See through the eyes of victory and not defeat. Live from victory not looking for victory. The victorious life for you is right now as your eyes and mind are being enlightened with a wealth of wisdom, knowledge and understanding.

~Pastor Turkeisa Rushin

Word of Prayer & Affirmation

Thank You Lord! Father, in the name of Jesus, thank you. Thank your for opening my eyes, renewing my mind, filling the holes in my soul and introducing me to promises that were hid from me. I receive the blessings of the new covenant that comes with better promises. I repent for being distracted with myself and others. I receive healing from all emotional imbalances right now. I renounce all legal and illegal covenants working against me, my life, my family, my finances, my ministry, my property and my possessions. I activate my restitution as you recompense me of loss and wasted years in time. I am exercising my faith at this moment of recovery and I choose to stay connected to the vine. I welcome the pruning and the purging needed for my life and my forward progressive motion. I send destruction to all fruits, seeds, deeds, tendencies and roots of wickedness and unrighteousness working in me or through me and around me. I declare and decree much fruit, fruits of righteousness, success and favor shall cover my life. As I am strengthened, encouraged empowered and established, I will and shall return and strengthen the brethren. Lord, I am eternally grateful and shall continually bless your Holy name. Let your eyes and ears be attentive to the prayer made in this place right now perpetually. In Jesus Name I pray, Amen.

Scriptural references:

The Nelson Study Bible, NKJV. 1997, Thomas Nelson, Inc. used by permission.

Seek Release– No More Excuses

To those with aspirations but no inspiration, unction but lack the faith to function, zeal but struggle with selfish wills, instructions but lack directions, vision but limited resources and to those seemingly with a word but no listeners …**THIS IS FOR YOU!**

We have an adversary that has a skillfully crafted and unmerciful ministry to kill, steal and destroy. To those who are ignorant (in the dark) of his devices, he wins continuously, relentlessly, generationally and religiously without always breaking rules but mostly following the rules that we as Christians and saints ignore.

Many are focusing on people as the enemy, adversary and opponent. In reality, the people (you and I included) have been instruments and tools of both good and evil at some point or another. So coming out, overcoming, breaking through, surviving and moving forward has to start in the individual. Hurt, pain, rejection, disappointment, hopelessness, fear, unbelief, doubt, shame, indecisiveness and trauma affect the human soul very deeply.

It takes a made up mind, much patience, love, care and wise counsel while seeking the Lord consistently to even begin to see the break of day. Blaming others becomes convenient and easy. Praying becomes harder and listening becomes boring so now hope seems lost. **WRONG!** That's the perfect time to tap into faith and believe even when believing seems hopeless and useless. *No more excuses!* Let us pray…

"Lord, I come to you seeking counsel, forgiveness, understanding, healing and love. I willingly renounce and fall out of agreement with the plan of failure working

against my life. I renounce my selfish will and desires, stubborn tendencies and my own inward self-destructive seeds, unfruitful memories, thoughts, feelings and emotions. Jesus come into my heart that I may know the Father through you. I repent for putting any and everything before you. I thirst and hunger for righteousness right now. Let me taste and see your goodness. Wash me and cleanse me. Lead me and guide me. Sprinkle my consciousness with the blood of the Lamb. I desire to know your will and I choose to follow you. I freely open my heart, mind, body and soul for new birth, new life and complete healing through the power of the Holy Ghost. You are my Savior and Lord. To you I surrender all. In Jesus Name, Amen."

Now your task begins and the fires shall surely come to try your faith but you already have access to all you need to stand. You have the full armor of God, the armor of love, your robe of righteousness and your garments of salvation. The Lord is your righteousness and you have been sealed with the Holy Ghost of promise. The process is just the moment to prepare for the end result. You have to tell yourself, "I will not die in this moment," and continue to feed your situation the word of God believing that He is and is a *rewarder* to those who diligently seek Him, the Lord. Another simple prayer, **"Lord I believe but help my unbelief"**.

For everything that comes up, there is a prayer. Unsuccessful cycles are destroyers to oppress your mind, keep you aware of hurts, pains, disappointments and bad decisions. It is time to confront the cycles of your life so that you can experience the Greater with no regrets. Let's make no more excuses!

The gospel of Matthew, Mark and Luke tell of the story of a boy healed. The father took him to the disciples for help but they could not heal him. The bible records when the lad saw Jesus as he was going to him, the spirit manifested. In **Mark**, Jesus asked the father how long he had been like this and the father replied, "Since childhood." The unseen sources to unsuccessful cycles in the lives of many today are rooted in events that occurred in childhood. It's time to take it to Jesus and stop suppressing it.

If you knew that you possessed what was needed to deal with it you would have done it already but you don't believe. Some things truly can only be dealt with through tedious and spirit led fasting and prayer. If only you could believe. "All things are possible to him who believes," is what Jesus said to the boy's father. The seizing, demonic mute spirit, kept the boy from speaking but yet bruised him, caused him to fall in the fire and water, and even foam at the mouth. Today, we are tossed to and fro, unable to speak, and convulsed from overwhelming events but unable to properly display emotion to them in self-defense. Hence, the proper resolve is not reached.

Whatever and whoever has silenced you and taken away your voice is losing power over your life right now. Even as you read the words on this page strength is coming to you to confront, dismiss and recover. Faith is increasing to produce the God-like results that you deserve in your everyday life. Let us pray…

"Lord, today I acknowledge the silence that has hindered me from events and times past. No longer shall I be ruled, tormented and crippled by my lack of faith. As I begin to trust you in my journey of fasting and praying, I desire to be free in Christ Jesus. I know life has more to offer me than what I have been introduced to. Today I receive all things new. I open up the gift of faith in my life and activate the spirit of faith for my life. I choose to follow Jesus and learn of Him that I may recover all and keep myself in right

standing with the Lord. I am acknowledging my ignorance and embracing the knowledge, wisdom, understanding and self-control needed to remain in the faith. Today, right now, all unsuccessful cycles are over in my life. I receive restoration mentally, physically, spiritually, financially and relationally. I am healed. I am whole. I am redeemed. In Jesus Name, Amen."

Be free from condemnation, regrets and your past. If you choose to forgive yourself and others, you will do well. Many of the answers to common dilemmas today are hidden in plain sight in the very scriptures quoted but not lived. What you have done is not who you are. You are a child of the free woman not the bondwoman. I pray that you embrace the perfect law of liberty which is the law of love, **James 1:25**. Also reflect on **John 8:32, 36-38** and **Galatians 5:13**.

Seize the moment to be accountable, strengthened, trusted, forgiven, directed and healed. All of these work for you and shows your growth in Christ Jesus. The desire to grow should be as evident as the air you breathe, a necessity as proof of life. Live I say. Live. Your best days are ahead of you and your worst days are behind you. Maximize the moment to be free and walk as a child of the light in whom no darkness can be found. You deserve it! No more Excuses!

PASTOR *Turkeisa Rushin* is the founder and pastor of *Empowerment Temple, Inc.* located in Cuthbert, Ga. She is the wife of Delton Rushin and mother of Keychard, Keshaun, Khalar, Kwandarius and Tyreak.

Pastor Rushin is a fulltime nurse for special needs children through a private duty agency and loves the ministry opportunity that her job provides as she enters these children's lives to provide skilled nursing care.

Pastor Rushin is a native of Cuthbert, Ga but currently resides in Albany, Ga. Her passion for souls is stirring up the hope that so many had lost and are now empowered to believe again. Pastor Rushin strives to advance the kingdom, one soul at a time.

Pastor Turkeisa Rushin

Church Mailing Address *

Empowerment Temple, Inc.
PO Box 4103 Albany, Ga 31701

Church Location *

329 Fourth Street Cuthbert, Ga 39840

Cell * 229-854-9541

Email *   kcrushin2006@gmail.com

"Rise Up and Shine,

for your light…"

Isaiah 60: 1

Rise Above Adversity–
The 5 'Gets' To Get In The Flow

God promised the children of Israel a land flowing with milk and honey just as He has given us promises. When Moses sent the 12 spies to scout out the land that God had promised them, 10 spies (83%) came with a negative report saying, "All the people that we saw in it are men of a great stature. And there we saw the giants…and we were in OUR own sight as grasshoppers and so we were in THEIR sight." Only 2 spies (17%) came with a positive report saying "Let us go up at once and possess it; for we are WELL able to overcome it. "

They saw the same thing, yet their perception was different - not at what they saw on the outside but what they saw on the inside. From that I learned that there are two kinds of people in this world. Those that see the obstacle as an

opportunity to excel and those that see
the obstacle as an object for excuse.

Those that excel and those that
excuse get the same obstacles but their
perception of who they are is different.
When told, 'you can't do that' or 'it has
never been done' or 'why are you
wasting your time on that - nothing is
going to come of it', those that excel use
those words to propel them to a level
that is not only efficient but effective.
Those that excuse use those words as an
excuse NOT to really tap into their
potential and allow it to lie dormant
within them.

If YOU are going to get in the flow
it starts with YOU. YOU are the
deciding factor. I have five 'Gets' that
YOU must get to help YOU, *Get in the
flow*:

GET out of the ordinary.
If you really want to get in the flow
you must get out of the ordinary. You
must get out of the familiar and what

you consider normal and comfortable. You must break out of the *status quo* of ordinary for you. When you are faced with a challenge of change it is very easy to want to revert back to what you know and what feels comfortable to you - your comfort zone. In this time that small still voice, if you allow it, will be consumed by the familiarity of what's been.

Insanity is doing the same thing over and over and expecting the results to be different. If you live according to what others think then you'll never live. Don't allow or let other people's opinions bind, shackle, deter, sabotage, control, manipulate or cancel out the visions, dreams, desires or aspirations of God that He placed in your heart.

The very existence of your gifts, talents and abilities should be validation because they are tools that God has equipped you with to help you walk, reach and fulfill your destiny. You are not a fleeting thought in the mind of

God but a carefully calculated well thought out one.

In the essence of who God is, not only did God speak His mind, He masterfully and purposely carries it out through His greatest creation - man. His greatness and purpose are locked deep within you. Let your naysayers and haters motivate and push you to your blessings. Let your enemies upgrade you.

That's what defines you and takes you from mediocrity to excellence and greatness. Don't let what people say or do build barricades or imprison your destiny. Don't devalue what God has placed in you because of circumstances or situations that you are going through or people's opinions. Don't allow those circumstances, situations or opinions alter or abort your God given visions, dreams and destiny to think that you can't.

Release your faith and rise above all doubts. Don't allow anyone to box you, your gifts, talents, abilities or resources or limit your potential. Don't allow anyone to dictate what you can or cannot do. You set the parameters. You set the boundaries. *If you continue to do what you've always done, you will continue to get what you've always gotten.* It's time to do something different. It's time to get out of the ordinary. It's time to enlarge your capacity, lengthen your borders and strengthen your cords. Miraculous things happen for those who step out of their complacency and comfort and begin to walk in faith.

GET out of the same old thinking.

Our mindset is the number one cause of hindrance. When our minds are trapped in impoverished thinking, slave mentality, idle thinking, lazy thinking, negative thinking or pity party thinking, we position ourselves to be stuck in the same place. You must control the thoughts that you allow to take residence in your mind. The only thing stopping you from reaching your full potential is your thinking.

The thoughts and fears that you have are formed from your past experience. You stop watching the reruns of your past, live stream your present and watch the previews of your future. Do not let what happened stop you one more day. You are in the fight for your destiny. You must step out of the boat and trust God!

It's the enemy's job to use the circumstances and situations that have devastated and depleted your confidence to discourage you. If you stay discouraged long enough it will soon lead to depression. Your thoughts or way of thinking can often times clog the flow that you desire to experience due to thoughts of fear, doubt, unbelief, etc.

Thoughts can alter and/or affect your actions. If you want a greater flow you must raise your lever of consciousness of thinking. If you want to change you must go to the root which are your thoughts. Fighting the good fight of faith is not only warfare against the devil but also in your mind. This is an ongoing fight. The mind controls the seat of your emotions. How you think is how you will feel and eventually act.

GET *rid of the clutter*.

When I think of clutter I think of it as useless and unnecessary things, people or situations that people cling to that are insignificant to their life and adds no value. One of the things I have discovered in life is that you never know how much stuff you have accumulated until you get ready to move. It's then that you begin to find the unnecessary things that you needed at one time but no longer need, however are still hanging on to.

The problem is that we like to move junk or clutter from one place to another. We want to hold on to it because we will never know when we will 'need' it again. But what we don't realize is that though the clutter was *once* useful, it has served its purpose. Once it has served its purpose there is no use for it anymore. We must take inventory of our lives through the leading of the Holy Spirit and being to clean out the unnecessary things, people and situations that are blocking us from getting the bountiful blessings and experiencing the greater in God.

GET rid of the toxicity.

One of the most dangerous things is to have a flow but for it be toxic. The devil comes to kill, steal and to destroy and he uses people, things or situations to do it. You must rid yourself immediately of toxicity for it is hazardous to flow.

GET *over it!*

One of the most tragic situations that a person can encounter is being stuck in time as time moves on. It's like wearing an outfit that you have obviously outgrown. It looks silly and others will chuckle yet so many are living that truth emotionally:

- *You're loved one died and you stopped living.*
- *Someone broke your heart and you can't seem to put the pieces back together.*
- *You made bad choices or decisions.*
- *You feel you can no longer fulfill the desires of your heart.*
- *You lost everything.*
- *Life was good and then it took a wrong turn.*
- *No one would help you, now you are bitter.*

Yes, each one of the above examples is a painful and hurtful situation, however you can't stay there and only exist in this world. You must move past that and live. You can get over it. You can begin again starting now.

When I say "Get over it!" I am not saying that to belittle or make light of what you have been through. I am merely pointing out to you that there is so much more than what you are holding on to. God is there to help you through every situation if you allow Him to.

As you begin to put these 5 'Get's' into action I believe you will not only *Get in the flow,* but you will experience a great outpouring of God. Walk in it. Keep it flowing. Don't let anybody, anything or any situation clog your flow.

~Elder Gerry Wootson

ELDER *Gerry L. Wootson*

(Minister, Poet & Songwriter) has been writing since the age of thirteen. He has overcome many obstacles in life such as a learning disability that was discovered in the 2nd grade.

It was then that he was told that he would not be anybody nor amount to anything. He was told he'd never read past a sixth grade level nor graduate from high school. However, through hard work, determination, dedication, supportive parents and an unshakeable faith in God, he went on to defy the odds.

Elder Gerry L. Wootson accepted Christ as his Lord and personal Savior in November 1992. He preached his initial sermon in October 2007 and was ordained in October 2008.

Elder Wootson has been called and anointed by God to preach God's Word. He established *Wootson Ministries* in 2010 to minister to hurting humanity and speak to the purposes of God within and encourage them to walk in their God given destiny and reach their God given potential through the preached and taught word, books, CDs, poetry, etc.

Although quiet in nature, Elder Wootson stands tall to declare the truth of God. "It's the truth," says Wootson "that makes us free."

He credits his parents, Elder Johnnie and Carrie Wootson for training him in the admonition of the Lord. Elder Wootson faithfully serves as an associate minister at *Overflow International Church Ministry* with Pastor Charlie A. Connor III and First Lady Michelle Connor. He also serves as President of the *Communications Ministry*. He resides in Richmond, Virginia with his wife Tamara.

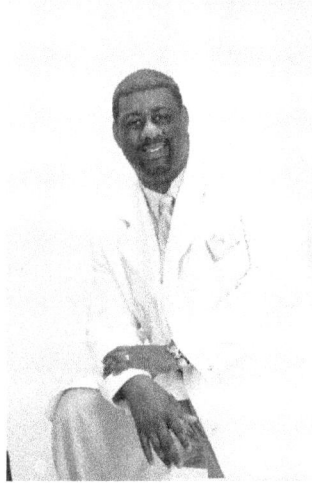

Elder Gerry L. Wootson

P.O. Box 71761
Henrico VA 23255

Phone * 804-852-8599

YouTube *
www.youtube.com/gwootson

Facebook * Elder G

Twitter * ElderG

Email * gwootson73@gmail.com

Rise Above Disappointment– Your Child Has Autism

Nearly 32 years ago, I was blessed with a gift that I had little knowledge of just how big the blessing would become. What do you do when the doctor tells you, *"Your child has autism,"* and you do not know what that means or what it is?

I had many questions like, 'Why,' 'How did it happen,' and 'Will he grow out of this?' One thing is for certain, your life is set on a different course now than before your baby was born!

I set out on a quest to find answers to my many questions. During those years the diagnosis was so new that they determined that only one in 10,000 were diagnosed with autism. And you guessed it we were the next!

Marc was the subject of many research projects as this new phenomenon was introduced to life.

We have many fond stories as well as grave ones as we trekked on this journey, but nevertheless, the joy of it all has outweighed any distresses we encountered.

Now my marriage did not survive the stress of this new life, but I did! And with this new life, I found that the most important thing to do was learn how to have balance as I had two other children to care for as well: An older daughter, (of whom I am very proud of and who works in social services) and a younger son (a Tuskegee graduated engineer who teaches beginning engineering and makes me equally as proud). They both love and adore their brother and are always interested in what he does next – which is a lot!

Below are a couple of encounters that I thought were adorable to share from my journal of him:

Today Marc kept leading me to a spot in his room. I picked up one thing then another, didn't know what he wanted. Later during the day he came to me again, this time I picked up some white skinny jeans that his brother bought him - that was it! He took his position on the bed where I dress him daily! I laughed so-o hard then I promised to put them on him tomorrow. NOW HE IS PICKING OUT HIS CLOTHES!!!! He is so cute.

***** *Get In The Flow* *****

Marc and I graced a local bread shop with our presence today. It was a task trying to stand in line to order him something to eat so that I could get on the Internet. The funniest thing happened when one of the waiters said "he's visiting," I ran over only to find Marc sitting with this couple and waiting to eat the man's food...I made apologies and dismissed us. The lady was kind and said that he was going to dine with them...I thought – poor lady if you only knew Marc will eat ALL of your food! Too Funny!

Although it has been one long journey making it to this point, we have endured the learning process as well as the acceptance process and now we just enjoy our lives with each other. Has this been hard? Yes! Through lots of learning to fast and pray we have made it. I learned to stand on God's promises, for example: "...he will never leave you nor forsake you," **Deuteronomy 31: 6** and realizing that I was one of God's chosen people such as those mentioned in **Colossians 3: 12** along with other such scriptures have made it possible for me to grow to where I am today.

Now that I have overcome many of the issues faced with having and caring for a child with special needs, I am arming myself to be able to help others physically as well as spiritually. Because we must know that caring for someone who depends totally on us is no easy feat and that you must learn to be armed with the love of God, the

Word of God and the Spirit of God, each day! Without Him it is all impossible.

Yes some people can manage but have you ever noticed those who have short fuses, always snapping at people or situations? They are not relying on God to be their source: source of energy, source of strength or source of comfort.

It may all sound easy enough to do but victory comes with a hefty price of fasting and praying and quiet time with our Holy Master. Exercise your Spiritual muscles as you do your physical muscles – the results are much more rewarding!

As I encounter new avenues for my son in my quest of a great quality of life for him, you see, I am planning for his life in the event I leave him first. I want his daily life to be such that, someone (his brother or sister) can pick up and run with it as though they are reading a book. Thank You Jesus!

Below is an example of an initiative I proposed to some business leaders which would benefit not only my son but the population of special needs citizens in one area of Dallas:

1. The purpose of this initiative is to offer an alternative day program to families of citizens with special needs in the Dallas-Ft. Worth areas in lieu of institutionalized facilities. This program provides a place that is as loving and warm as a home environment yet complete with stimulating and learning activities.
2. The day habilitation program provides families with quality care for their love one during the day whether it is due to work or a brief respite care relief for a few hours. This day program will work in cooperation with the Texas MHMR program as a referral for needed clients.

I have the prior knowledge and experience needed to operate this type of program because I am the mother of a child who has Autism and needs daily care for the rest of his life. He has been a client in a much needed day habilitation program since graduating high school.

Some individuals with special needs are capable of going beyond high school to employment and for some, even college. However, there is an even larger population who simply need daily care. I have established such a day habilitation program to service my son's needs as well as the needs of other such citizens in the Dallas-Fort Worth area.

As we take this venture, parents or caregivers would be able to work longer days if they so choose. Still others will be able to enjoy a night out on the town or simply a relaxing dinner out without the worries, having the confidence that their loved one is safe and secure. These are constant concerns of a parent anyway but all the more magnified when the child is actually an adult who needs to be cared for as a child.

So as one can see my blessings
have been even more than I could
imagine since hearing those four words,
"Your child has Autism." He is such a
joy in many ways and very smart.
Autistic individuals internalize
everything and then only reveal that
part of them that they want you to see.

Marc chooses not to talk, although
he has used some speech in the past. He
understands verbal directions and
commands well but may choose not to
comply. We speak for him so much that
I believe he thinks it to be cute not to.
At moments you can see him being
involved in his surroundings then other
times he will withdraw to what we
commonly term as "having an autistic
moment." He loves music in any form
and even sings and dances.

The thing that is most fascinating is
that his discernment of people is very
keen. It reminds me of scripture in

Revelations where those who have not been tainted by the world will follow Jesus around … "These are they." Thank you God that Marc is in that category! Now it is up to us to make sure we can be in Jesus' presence as being forgiven.

Thank you God for this opportunity and sheer pleasure to share our experiences with others. It is with hope and prayer that it will be a help and a blessing to all who reads this.

~Gena Irby Hill

SISTER *Gena Irby Hill* is an Alabama Native who now resides in Dallas, TX, is a self-proclaimed artist who creates and designs pictures and other artistic designs and a past Educator who took early retirement to care for her son full-time.

Gena accepted Christ at an early age and now dedicates her life to intercessory prayer full-time.

Gena Irby Hill

Phone * 469-952-4723

Email * genairby@yahoo.com

Rise Above Opposition-
Opposition Didn't Stop What God Has Destined

As a very young child I dealt with many years of being tormented. Things were happening to me that I couldn't quite comprehend. Unlike the average child, I found myself at a very early age trying to look deep within my soul. I would ask myself questions such as, "Who am I? Why am I here? And who made me?" Being unable to answer those questions I found myself clueless about my identity and my purpose in life. I remember standing in front of the mirror staring, looking deeply within my eyes for long periods of time. I would stare at the mirror for such an extended amount of time until I would black out and end up passing out onto the floor.

The easiest prey is a child. A child does not have the ability to fight. Shortly after this episode, I had an encounter with a demonic spirit. I can vividly remember being tormented by them. I dealt with spirits that would tell me that I wouldn't live to be eighteen. I even heard them tell me they were going to kill me. These spirits had such a hold on me. I would break out with sores that would cover my entire body. I also encountered an episode where my tongue literally was pulling to the back of my throat!

At the age of nine-years-old I was tormented to the point the doctors decided to admit me to a psychiatric hospital. Can you image that? I was HORRIFIED! Two weeks later I was released after showing no signs of mental impairment.

A day or so later, I was prayed for and introduced to this man named JESUS! He saved me, delivered me and set me free. I was snatched out of the hand of the enemy. I am thankful for His grace and mercy. God turned it! Satan's plans didn't work. HE NEVER WANTED ME TO BE INTRODUCED TO THE SAVIOR.

God has exposed the enemy's strategies and attacks. The Bible teaches that I am an overcomer and this is a daily task. Being more than a conqueror always places me with the victory. The five foolish virgins and the five wise virgins had to go through a season of listening to the beckoning call of the father. **Romans 8:28** reads, "And we know that all things work together for good to them that love God, to them who are the called according to his purpose."

There's a purpose behind your problem. God's purpose in time of trouble is to teach us. It is to educate and build us up. I am overly excited that it worked out for me. Once I gave my life to the Lord Jesus, the enemy became defeated and he is currently under my feet. I thank Him for His deliverance and restoration in every area of my life. I continue to totally surrender to the Lord and to His perfect will for my life.

The enemy wants to instill the spirit of fear in our lives. It is his goal to weaken our spirit of faith and manifest hopelessness and depression. You are vulnerable unless you claim the gift of grace which is Jesus Christ. I am convinced that there is power in the name of Jesus. **John 10:10** reads, "The thief cometh not, but for to steal, kill and destroy: I am come that they might have life and that they might have it more abundantly."

This scripture became a part of me and gave me life. For me to find out that Jesus didn't come to destroy but to give me life gave me GREAT JOY! Giving life is the greatest gift ever. God can give life to your dead situation. I finally came into the knowledge of truth about some things. The more I went to church the more scriptures I started memorizing.

Pondering on those scriptures helped me get rooted in my spirit and has helped me establish a true walk in Christ Jesus.

Be alert, be on watch. **I Peter 5:8** reads, "Be sober, be vigilant; because your adversary the devil, as a roaring lion, walketh about, seeking whom he may devour:" Satan waits like a lion and attacks us when we are at our most vulnerable stages of life. It is the devil's job to try and distract us from our destiny. Another scripture to keep in mind is **Ephesians 6:12**. "For we wrestle not against flesh and blood, but against principalities, against powers, against the rulers of the darkness of this world, against spiritual wickedness in high places."

There is wickedness all around and it's our responsibility to cover the next generation. It is so important to pray and cover our children in the blood of Jesus and teach them the ways of the lord. It is vital to "Train up a child in the

way he should go: and when he is old he will not depart from it." **Proverbs 22:6** "You shall teach them diligently to your children and shall talk to them when you sit in your house and when you walk by the way and when you lie down and when you rise."
Deuteronomy 6:7. The effects of attack or abuse may linger around but Jesus has promised to set us free. Some may never find deliverance if they never allow Christ to come into the dark places of their lives.

Demons can assume beguiling appearances that easily lead people astray. Therefore it's important that we remain in the word of God and obey Jesus. Believers know that demons are in fact doomed. Christ has defeated Satan. He knows his time is short therefore he is doing everything in his power to destroy God's people.

Demonic spirits are running rapid in our new age generation therefore let's intercede for them and our nation as a whole. We need the power of God to raise our children. "Watch ye therefore and pray always, that ye may be accounted worthy to escape all these things and shall come to pass." **Luke 21:36**

There is power in the name of Jesus. Years ago when my daughter was nine-years-old she dealt with some demonic issues. To my amazement, she had been similarly attacked as I had been. I thank God that I was able to recognize and help her fight this spiritual battle.

Two of your most powerful defenses are: The name of Jesus and the blood of Jesus. I had a vision three months ago. In my vision I was asleep on my bed and I saw this black shadow standing over me. As I squinted in fear the evil spirit began touching me and I began to yell "The blood of JESUS!" The spirit instantly left me. "Therefore also God highly exalted Him, and bestowed on Him the name which is above every name that at the name of Jesus every knee shall bow, of those who are in heaven and, on earth and under the earth, and that every tongue should confess that Jesus Christ is Lord, to the glory of God the father." **Philippians 2:9-11**

So in short, every knee must bow to the name of Jesus. "Submit yourselves therefore to God. Resist the devil, and he will flee from you." **James 4:7** You have the power to defeat the opposition. Get in position. I am delighted to write my testimony. It has developed and enhanced me as a person. These things did not break or kill me but they strengthened my innermost being of soul, body and spirit. I am a living witness of His grace, mercy, faithfulness and His love. I've tried Him and I know Him. He is: My King, My God, My Father ... My Testimony.

~Valerie Ramos

SISTER *Valerie Ramos*, 35, is a woman of faith, intercessor and servant. She is a woman who loves God. God is her first priority and she aims to please him.

Valerie loves supporting and assisting others. Her vision is to reach beyond the walls of the church and to not be complacent or self-centered, but to actively reach out and follow the mandate of Jesus. "Go ye into the entire world and preach the gospel to every creature." **Mark 16:15**

Valerie Ramos

Phone * 870-692-5060

Email * valerieramos10@yahoo.com

Email * Valerieramos401@yahoo.com
and Instant Tax Services.

Entrepreneurship Insurance Agent,
Licensed Energy Broker for Ignite,
builttolast.mystream.biz Asante
Executive, for
Asante Organic and Instant Tax
Services.

Rise above Fear–
Believe and Trust God

Praise God our Heavenly Father and His Son, Jesus Christ, our Lord and Savior. Surely the name of the Lord is a strong high tower that the righteous run into and are saved!

I give God praise because of His awesome presence in the lives of His Saints! He is our protector and He watches over us. Truly He never sleeps and He never slumbers as the scripture declares.

My husband was a long-distance truck driver and would be on the road as many as eight to ten days at time. I recall a time when he was away, I was seven months pregnant and my seven-year old son and niece were asleep in the next room.

I routinely checked to make sure that doors and windows were locked before going to bed and that's when I noticed that the sliding glass patio door would not latch properly. I tried using a broom and then a mop to stop the door from sliding open (that was all I had), but they were too short.

Since my husband wouldn't be home until the next day, I tried to force the lock to latch (even though it was not very secure) and went to bed for the night thinking we would be okay having prayed that God would keep us safe.

I'm not sure how long I had been asleep, when I heard the voice of an angel standing at the head of my bed urging me to get up and pray. I woke up to the words, "Arise daughter of Zion and pray! Believe God and pray!"

We had a 4 ½-ft Cox fence around the backyard and gates on each side of the house. The back portion of the yard had a 10-ft brick wall that separated the condominium community behind our neighborhood. The gates squeaked when opening so I always knew when the children were going in and out of the backyard while playing. My bedroom window was near the gate.

Just then I saw in a vision a man coming down my street. He was just passing the house next door. I saw this man plainly and heard him mumbling to himself in the vision God showed me of him. I quickly arose and kneeled down to pray. I immediately asked the Holy Spirit to help me to pray as I ought, as I wanted to ensure my faithful obedience to what the angel was telling me to do.

While praying and asking God to help me, I continued to see him in the vision and he turned into my yard from the sidewalk. I actually heard him walking through the grass on the side of my house. I tried very hard to focus on praying in spite of what I was seeing and hearing. The angel kept saying "Pray, pray, pray and believe God!"

I had hedges along the side and back of the house at my bedroom and bathroom. I saw him, in the vision, try to part the hedges and peer through my bedroom window at the same time I heard the edges pushing against the screen.

The angel said "A murdering spirit." And told me to trust God. The man could not see in my window as the curtains were closed. I then saw him approach the gate and open it and I heard the gate squeaking as it opened. I knew he was in the backyard and I remembered the latch was not very secure on the patio door.

Fear tried to enter in, but the angel said "Daughter of Zion, pray and believe God!" I felt the spirit of prayer overtake me and I became consumed in prayer. As I cried out to God with all my heart, I heard the voice of the angel moving and I looked up from praying on the side of my bed and saw the angel had left my bedside and was standing at the door with a sword drawn, holding it high in the air ready to strike.

I looked at the bedroom door and there was an electrical outlet in the hall where I kept a dim nightlight burning so the children could go to the bathroom during the night. I could see his legs darken the light as he walked pass it and stood at my bedroom door. I knew I was not seeing him in the vision as I could see the light reflecting off of a big knife he was holding in his hand hanging down the side of his leg.

The Holy Spirit was praying through me and I heard the words being prayed as I looked at this person in my house. The angel told me again to "Believe and trust God." I closed my eyes as I heard the angel continue to say, "Pray and believe God," and I continued to pray as the spirit of prayer was upon me and I was consumed in prayer.

I no longer saw or heard the angel yet I felt the presence of the Lord so powerful in the room. I remembered the man but did not see him or have any vision of him. I remembered the children were asleep in the next room and fear tried to enter in that something was done to them by the man. I felt my knees burning as the carpet was cutting deeply into my knees from kneeling in prayer for so long and I tried to stand.

I jumped to my feet and immediately the angel was there and said to me, "Believe God - take your rest and trust Him. Take your rest and trust in Him." I thought to myself, "I do believe God and I will trust Him to do everything I cannot." I got under the covers trusting that God had taken care of my son and niece as He had taken care of me.

I awoke later than usual the next morning. As I looked around my bedroom, I felt such a peace and calmness in the room and it looked like a light cloud resting in the atmosphere. I remembered the children and got up to go see them. When I walked into the room, I expected pillows on the floor and covers half off the bed. Instead they were still fast asleep and the bed covers had been placed on them and folded back just below their shoulders. They had been tucked into bed!

I stood there weeping and thanking God for what He had done. His mercy and grace is so rich toward us and all we have to do is pray and believe Him and trust in Him with all our hearts. As I stood there, I heard this sound that was not familiar. Again, fear tried to enter in and I fought against it and chose to believe and trust God.

I turned out of the children's room and began walking toward the sound coming from the kitchen area. I looked into the rooms as I continued walking and no one was there. As I turned toward the patio, I saw the patio door and screen had been left wide open and the wind was whipping the curtain in an out of the door and was making the 'flapping' sound that I was hearing. I realized that when the man left my house, he had left the door wide open.

My husband arrived home later that day and I told him what had happened and that he needed to repair the door lock. He was not a believer then and could not understand what great mercy God had shown us.

I love the Lord and have learned to trust God even more in so many other circumstances that I have faced in my life. I rejoice in the Word of God and relish my times in prayer and communion with Him. I even get jealous of time spent with having to live in this world and deal with life's encounters, when all I want to do with this time is spend it in prayer and in the presence of the Lord. I often think of this time when I read **Psalm 27** and **91**, as these Words are alive in me.

To all that read this testimony, be encouraged and know that God keeps us and watches over us and His

protection and love for us is truly
beyond our comprehension.
    God bless and keep you,
        ~ Sister Cora Stevenson

SISTER *Cora Stevenson* lives in her hometown of Dallas, Texas. She has three brothers and three sisters who also love the Lord. Cora moved to Orlando, FL in 1981 where she married and raised her three children. She has three grandchildren and a host of nieces and nephews.

God saved Cora and filled her with the gift of the Holy Ghost in July 1973 during a Friday night church service. "I truly love the Lord for His mercy and His grace in my life. God has truly been good to me. I praise the Lord, Jesus Christ – my Savior, for my journey with Him and His sweet revelations that has made me to know Him in a very special way." Says Cora.

She is thankful for this opportunity to share with you the experiences and testimonies of the awesome power of God's presence in her life. She prays that God richly blesses and keeps you.

Cora Stevenson

Facebook * cora.stevenson.75

Email *
Corastevensonministry@yahoo.com

"Be Still and *Know* that I am God"

Psalm 46:10

Know God—
My Prayer for My Mind

Hello, my name is Cora Stevenson and I am so excited to share this word of encouragement. God is so good and so very mindful of us. I thank Him for His love, His protection and providence and for His promises to those who love Him and are called according to His Will.

God has made me to know just how real He is and that He intervenes in our lives to teach, guide and protect us, as well as reveal Himself to us through all of life's experiences. I am humbled and so honored to share this testimony with you.

This prayer happened for me during a time of separation from my husband after being together for 17 years. We were definitely headed for divorce and I was trying to get through this trial as faithfully and courageously as I could. Upon arriving to work each morning, I would always say a prayer for my employer, co-workers and the daily work processes as my computer booted up for the day.

As I prayed, the Holy Spirit spoke to me saying, "Pray for your mind." This was a topic one of the ministers at my church had spoken on earlier that week. I immediately asked the Holy Spirit to help me pray this prayer, as I should, in order to be obedient to what the Spirit was telling me to do. I began scrambling for words to pray regarding my mind. At that point I heard and felt words being placed into my spirit and realized it was the work of the Holy Spirit and not me or my words.

My computer had completed booting up, so I started typing the words as I heard them - with no punctuation – just straight typing out the words as they flowed into my spirit. Once the words stopped, I read the words and completed the punctuation and paragraphing of what I had typed. I prayed the prayer as my prayer and printed a couple of copies.

One of my coworkers arrived just as I completed printing. She looked so tired and worn and wore a look of defeat on her face. I was still in the spirit and felt such a strong presence of God. We spoke and as she looked at me. I told her I had something I wanted to share with her and handed her a printed copy of the prayer.

She read it and was so encouraged by it! Her whole demeanor changed and I could see that her spirit was so lifted up! She hung the prayer on the wall near her desk and said she would pray this every day. I knew exactly how she felt, as this prayer had so encouraged me as well.

The receptionist was an older and very graceful woman and she had been with the company since its early years - at least 25 or more years. She and I would go to lunch together from time to time and I knew she loved the Lord, so I decided to share this prayer with her as well. I went downstairs to her desk and gave her a copy.

When I returned to my desk, one of the managers was at my desk reading the prayer I had left on my copyholder. He smiled at me and said, "Wow, this is good stuff!" We briefly talked about the goodness of God and he went back into his office.

I went to lunch late that day and noticed that the receptionist had the prayer sitting in a frame on her desk! She had purchased an 8x10 picture frame for it when she went to lunch earlier.

I have prayed many, many times as the Holy Spirit led me, but this is a very special prayer for me and has been with me since June 1999. I even mailed and emailed copies of this prayer to my family who lived out-of-state in hopes that it would encourage them as much as it had encouraged me.

Subsequently, I moved back to my home state and was visiting my sister at her home. I was so elated to see that she had a small 5x7 frame of this prayer sitting on her vanity and she told me how it yet encourages her. It was such a blessing to see how this prayer impacted her life as much as it had mine.

In all these years since God gave me this prayer – these words - to pray, I understand more and more why. God continues to affirm the words of this prayer and His Word in me and in my life.

My God-Given Prayer:

"Dear Father God, In the name of Jesus, hide me and keep me in your Word – Jesus Christ - my Lord and Savior that the spirit of my mind be renewed each day. Holy Spirit be in the recesses of my mind to give me wisdom, knowledge, understanding and strategy to war against the strongholds of iniquity and to fight the "Fight of Faith." And there also, let prayer and praise to the true and living God and to His glory abide." Amen.

Since my born-again experience in Christ, I understand more and more that God is truly my Heavenly Father. God has made me to know that He has always been there to make a difference in my life, even as a young girl and before I was drawn to Christ according to His Will to be saved, God protected me and kept me safe. He spoke to my heart and told me He loved me. Jesus is the Way that I enter into God's presence through the power of the Holy Ghost and faith in Christ.

In the Word of God, which is Jesus, am I hidden and kept - delivered from my enemies - even from the deceitful lusts of my own flesh and the carnality of my mind. The Word truly renews my mind and cleanses me. By God's Word, which is both Spirit and Life and being filled with God's gift of the Holy Ghost, I have the power to know wisdom and strategy to war against strongholds and the courage to fight the Fight of Faith.

I have learned through the fellowship of Christ's suffering comes obedience and understanding. As I seek His face and choose to answer His call to higher levels of obedience, I follow on to know Him more and more. I found that in seeking Him with all my heart, He will give revelation knowledge of Himself and His kingdom. God wants us to know Him and Jesus Christ continues to declare Him to us through the Holy Ghost, as we walk this journey of life by faith.

It is my heart's desire to give God praise and to acknowledge Him in all things concerning me, to allow my life to glorify Him through every trial, tribulation and through every temptation that I encounter and to give Him the glory for all the victories He has given me, so that my ways are pleasing, acceptable and faithful to Him and that I know Him for myself. One of my favorite scriptures is **Jeremiah 9:23-**

24, as I truly want to know Him more and more.

~**Cora Stevenson**

SISTER *Cora Stevenson* lives in her hometown of Dallas, Texas. She has three brothers and three sisters who also love the Lord. Cora moved to Orlando, FL in 1981 where she married and raised her three children. She has three grandchildren and a host of nieces and nephews.

God saved Cora and filled her with the gift of the Holy Ghost in July 1973 during a Friday night church service. "I truly love the Lord for His mercy and His grace in my life. God has truly been good to me. I praise the Lord, Jesus Christ – my Savior, for my journey with Him and His sweet revelations that has made me to know Him in a very special way." Says Cora.

She is thankful for this opportunity to share with you the experiences and testimonies of the awesome power of God's presence in her life. She prays that God richly blesses and keeps you.

Cora Stevenson

Facebook * cora.stevenson.75

Email *
Corastevensonministry@yahoo.com

Know Who You Are-
More Than Just The Pastor's Wife

How many of you think that you are just the wife of a pastor? Some of us are more than just the pastor's wife. We not only have a responsibility in the church, some of us are mothers, grandmothers with other responsibilities. Some of you have small children. In order to teach children in the church, the pastor's children should be the examples of how children should act. "Train up a child in the way he should go; and when he is old, he will not depart from it." **Proverbs 22:6**

This is the way of the Lord. "He that spareth the rod hated his son: but he that loveth him chasteneth betimes." **Proverbs 13:24** Meaning, if you love your children you will correct them. So if you are a pastor's wife with children you must teach your children to be examples. You can't minister or teach on chastening or being obedient if your own children are not an example. If your child or children are obedient to you but not other people it could cause problems.

Being a pastor's wife, some of us think our children are better than other children. Never think your children are better – just know they are different. Never let your children tell a member, "You can't tell me nothing, this is my daddy's church." That is disrespectful and a disobedient spirit and that can be a hindrance to your ministry. Some people already feel that the pastor's children should be the just ones in the church, to do right and they are right. They are supposed to be that example. But they are also human too. Pastor's children look at other children and to them it seems like they are getting away with everything. But I would tell my children, "You are different and you are supposed to make a difference".

When you have children and they are what we call *stair steps* and you are trying your best to keep them in order, there is nothing worse than somebody saying, "I wish she would make them sit down and shut up," knowing that your hands are full. But they choose to get irritated and aggravated, instead of trying to help. That's when you are more than just the pastor's wife. You must sit there and deal with it without getting frustrated and stay in the right attitude and mindset. I've been there. My husband and I had seven children and I had to deal with these types of situations. I thank God that he blessed us to raise them the right way and today we are proud of all them. All glory and honor goes to God.

Some of us wives are working women, so our work doubles. Sometimes people may not want to give you credit for anything but as long as God gets the glory it doesn't matter about people, because it's all about

Jesus. Being a woman, wife and mother you may have to deal with people that think they own you. It's not easy but God didn't say it would be. People often fail to realize that we are more than just the pastor's wife. We go through too.

In 2001 our family had a house fire the week before Thanksgiving. We went through an experience that I never thought or dreamed of happening. That Wednesday night we had a beautiful service. After service my husband left to take his mom to Houston. Not four hours after he left, one of my daughters (a gospel music producer) was sitting at the foot of my bed when all of sudden we smelled a peculiar smell but we just ignored it. I turned over in the bed and put the covers over my head to prepare to go to sleep as normal. I told my daughter to lie down because she was drifting off to sleep. My grandchildren had already fallen asleep on the side of me. I had no idea that it was the smell that was putting them to sleep.

As I began to close my eyes, my son, who was in the dining room, came to my room and very calmly said, "Momma there's a fire at the front door." I jumped up and called on Jesus. By the time I made it from the bedroom to the living room the fire had already burned the front door and midway into the living room. I ran to grab the babies and the cordless phone and began dialing 911. All the while, I was still calling on the name of Jesus.

We all ran to the back door but it was stuck. One of our Godsons (we will never forget him) lived across the street. We called him and he came and had to kick the door in. We thought everybody was outside including our little dog, Vision. Then I remembered somebody was under the cover in one of the bedrooms. I went back inside and found one of my daughters sleep. Apparently the smoke had gotten to her. I was calling her name but she would not answer. I shook her until she finally said, "Mama what's wrong?" I told her to get up and come on because the house was on fire.

God is a protector. As soon as we got down the hallway the ceiling collapsed. God blessed us to make it out. We ran across the street and said, "Devil you are a liar. You thought you had us but we got away and that way is Jesus."

I thank God each and every day that he spared our lives. The devil wanted us to die but God said, "Live."

We all go through different things in life and we as pastor's wives should lift one another up. It's a shame to live in a town where the pastor's wives have certain *clicks*.
In this walk of life, we should all *click* together. Without the right attitude and mind of Christ pastor's wives can become a hindrance.

A lot of times people think that the pastor's wives don't go through anything. People may never know this, but pastor's wives really go through. But I thank God for knowing how to pray through to get to. I

In the year 2004 my daughter, Shantocqua Nakim Childress Major, went to glory at the age of twenty-two. My heart was broken and felt like it was ripped out. If it had not been for God, my family and church family, I would have literally lost my mind. I thank God for a sound mind. I have had a lot of life's 'ups and downs', but I am still standing with the help of God.

There were days I wanted to just disappear and crawl into bed and never get up. But God wouldn't let me do such a thing nor have a pity party. That's why when you go to give up and throw your hands up, you need to look up and ask God to help you with whatever you are going through.

As pastor's wives, we should lift up one another and pray for one another. Because whether you think so or not we need each other (Glory to His

Name!). Without a shadow of a doubt, we are *more* than just the pastor's wife!

~First Lady Evangelist Jeanette Childress

Words of Encouragement

"He giveth power to the faint; and to them that have no might he increaseth strength."
Isaiah 40:29

"And whether we be afflicted if is for your consolation and salvation, which is effectual in the enduring of the dame sufferings which we also suffer; or whether we be comforted, it is for your consolation and salvation."
2Corinthians 1:16

"Bear ye one another's burdens, and so fulfill the law of Christ."
Galatians 6:2

"Look not to every man on his own things, but to every man also on the things of others."
Philippians 2:4

"Not forsaking the assembling of ourselves together, as the manner if some is; but exhorting one another: and so much the more, as ye see the day approaching."

Hebrews 10:25

"I can do all things through Christ that strengtheneth me."

Philippians 4:13

"The Lord is the light and my salvation; whom shall I fear? The Lord is the strength of my life; of whom shall I be afraid?"

Psalms 27:1

"When the wicked, even mine enemies and my foes, came upon me to eat up my flesh, they stumbled and fell."

Psalms 27:2

"Though an host should encamp against me, my heart shall not fear: though war should rise against me, in this will I be confident."

Psalms 27:3

"One thing have I desired of the LORD, that will I seek after; that I may dwell in the house of the LORD all the days of my life, to behold the beauty of the LORD, and to enquire in his temple."

Psalms 27:4

"And now shall mine head be lifted up above mine enemies round about me: therefore will I offer in his tabernacle sacrifices of joy; I will sing, yea, I will sing praises unto the LORD."

Psalms 27:6

"Wait on the LORD: be of good courage, and he shall strengthen thine heart: wait, I say, on the LORD."

Psalms 27:14

"That ye might walk worthy of the Lord unto all pleasing, being fruitful in every good work, and increasing in the knowledge of God..."

Colossians 1:10

"Fear thou not; for I am with thee: be not dismayed; for I am thy God: I will strengthen thee; yea, I will help thee; yea, I will uphold thee with the right hand of my righteousness."

Isaiah 41:10

"He giveth power to the faint; and to them that have no might he increaseth strength."

Isaiah 40:29

"Wherefore take unto you the whole amour of God, that ye may be able to withstand in the evil day, and having done all, to stand."

Ephesian 6:13

"Counsel is mine, and sound wisdom: I am understanding; I have strength."

Proverbs 8:14

"The LORD is my rock, and my fortress, and my deliverer; my God, my strength, in whom I will trust; my buckler, and the horn of my salvation, and my high tower."

Psalms 18:2

"And said, O man greatly beloved, fear not: peace be unto thee, be strong, yea, be strong. And when he had spoken unto me, I was strengthened, and said, Let my lord speak; for thou hast strengthened me."

Daniel 10:19

1ST LADY *Evangelist Jeanette M. Childress* was born and raised in Houston, Texas - 5ᵗʰ Ward to be exact. She united in Holy Matrimony to the now Chief Apostle Lionel Childress Sr. they have 7 biological children, 10 grandchildren, plenty of God children and adopted ones as well.

After relocating to Marshall, TX in 1979, Lady Childress and her husband where faithful in other ministries until God spoke to them to start a church of their own. *Childress Deliverance Temple* became established in 1989 and has been growing stronger ever since.

Now Co-Pastor Lady Childress found herself working alongside of her husband filling in where ever she was needed. She wrote an in-house book called *The Pastors Wife* that has help several of the covenant 1ˢᵗ Ladies as well as mentoring others. She is a powerful singer, evangelist and praise & worship leader.

She is founder of *Morning Glory* giving ministers in training an opportunity to come and perfect their gifts and talents. She is straight forward, always loving and an understanding Woman of God!

First Lady Evangelist
Jeanette Childress

Facebook * Jeanette.childress.7

Know Your Worth–
The Beauty of Being a Woman

One of the greatest things God has ever done was when He created the woman. We are so uniquely and wonderfully made! God made woman beautiful and marvelous in his sight. From the beginning, we were put in a position to help. Naturally, we have taken on the attributes to help in every aspect of our lives. The scripture reads, "And the Lord God said, It is not good that the man should be alone; I will make him an help meet for him." **Genesis 2:18**. As the verses proceed we learn that God caused a deep sleep to come over Adam. God removed a rib out of Adam's side and created Eve. Just like God created Eve to be a help meet for Adam, he also created all other women to be a help meet. Some may ask, "How does this apply to the single woman?" Being a help meet in specific capacities is always necessary whether we are married or single. Also, knowing the significance of being a help meet is essential as it prepares the single woman for marriage.

As a woman I truly understand the value of being in my rightful place. But I didn't always have this testimony. Because I grew up being so independent, it was difficult for me to let my husband lead me. Often, I would overrule him in certain situations, speak harshly to him and was just blatantly disrespectful on a consistent basis. I felt justified being that I was the spouse with the higher income and even had more education. Sadly, many women in this country are in the same position in their marriages and also feel justified. Today is the day that type of thinking must change and we must understand that regardless of how much education we have or how much our paychecks are, we must continue to remain in our rightful places in our marriages.

Eventually, as time went on, I saw the love that my husband once had for me slowly deplete. I began to see him shut down and shut me out. When I finally realized what had taken place he was in a place of resentment. I sought out counseling and did whatever I could to let my husband see I had changed. It was like talking to walls. He was no longer there.

This does not have to be the fate of every woman. Women have the ability to lead in the workplace and simultaneously be a great wife and mother at home. I remember when I was in a place of trying to mature, I was careful about how I responded to my spouse and did my best to line up with the Word of God as to how a wife should respond to her husband. During one of the moments of trying to do right, one of my students asked my husband if I the boss at home? He laughed and told the student, "Not at all." The student said, "Well if she is running things here at the school, I am sure she does the same thing at home." I looked at the student and replied, "When I am at home I am his wife there is no need to do his job."

It is essential that we portray God's awesome work through our actions every day of our lives. God loves us so much, that he placed man to love and provide for us and treat us with love and kindness. The scripture gives the man a perfect remedy for loving on his wife. "Likewise, ye husbands, dwell with them according to knowledge, giving honor unto the wife, as unto the weaker vessel and as being heirs together of the grace of life; that your prayers be not hindered." **I Peter 3:7** This does not mean that women are weaker; it simply means that the husband ought to perform with tender and wise consideration towards the wife. The woman has to be wise enough to allow her husband to do this for her. A man takes pride in his bride looking to him for provision and protection as the woman should take pride in her husband desiring for her to be emotionally secure.

Some of the single ladies may ask the question, "Where are the good men?" Believe me, there are men who will treat you and love you as Christ loves the church. But what is so essential is that we first learn to love ourselves. Don't put men in a position where they have to constantly build you up due to lack of self-esteem. Women must look within and find out what are the things that make them happy. Also, if there are things that must be done to build self-esteem, we must not make excuses and just do it. Life can be so beautiful when you learn to love yourself. When a woman begins to love herself this attribute exudes confidence. When a woman is confident that in turn draws a man. The key is making sure you draw the right man.

Companionship, friendship, relationship… which will it be? The mind of a woman who desires to be loved thinks about the above categories sometime prematurely. Settling for the mediocrity a man portrays by just accepting a few calls a week and maybe hanging out every now and then is not sufficient.

All the signs are there. He's showing how he feels, but sometimes as women we can be so desperate we will continue to pursue. Buying him things and giving him things that he like will not turn his heart when his heart is not in it.

Often the woman is looking for a commitment and the man is looking for a good time. I think about the very direct words of my brother in a situation like this. He simply says, "That dude does not like you, face it." We can say, "That's harsh," but it's better for a woman to realize this early before getting to a point where it's too hard to let go.

One thing about a man, he will make time for the things that interest him. When a man is interested, you don't have to buy him anything - he's still there to pursue you. (Even in a man's pursuit, it's important that we understand that every man that pursues us is not for us.) It is vital as a woman to set a standard and seek God for direction versus seeking our fleshly desires for answers. It feels so good to be loved but it feels awesome when we let God send us who He has for us. The key is loving ourselves, remaining confident, keeping the faith, trusting God and eventually the right one will come.

Women were made to be help meets to the man and we were also made and have the ability to help ourselves. We possess so many attributes to add flavor to the world and we can do that and be loved by the man

God has chosen for us. **Proverbs 31:10-12** reads, "Who can find a virtuous woman? For her price is far above rubies. The heart of her husband doth safely trust in her, so that he shall have no need of spoil. She will do him good and not evil all the days of her life." Whether single or married we can all be virtuous, confident, beautiful women. We hold the key to our futures based off our desire to help and not rule.

~LaKeitha D. Givens

SISTER *LaKeitha D. Givens*

and Cedric Givens have four beautiful children together. Some say their children are beautiful but LaKeitha says hers really are (smile). She loves to smile and loves making education a wonderful experience. Mrs. Givens accepted Christ in her life as a teenager and has not looked back since. She loves continuing her efforts to build a close and genuine relationship with God and His people. She is a young lady who is studious about the Word of God!

Before being introduced to the environment of education, she attended Detroit College of Business where she obtained an Associate's Degree in Business Administration with an Accounting Emphasis. After much encouragement she continued her education, eventually obtaining her Bachelor's degree in Accounting specializing in Certified Public Accounting from Davenport University. In 2008, she finally earned her Masters of Accounting and Financial Management from Keller Graduate School of Management. Currently she is working to achieve her PhD in Organizational Leadership and Development.

After much schooling and working at a local hospital for 13 years, LaKeitha realized that education was her first love. She had been teaching and tutoring teenagers as well as college students for the past eight years. She truly found it gratifying helping others accomplish their educational goals. She started out working at a local middle school by providing embedded learning and exposing students to enrichment activities but was quickly promoted to coordinate programs for grades K-6 and eventually 7-12th grade.

Her school administration has summed up her work in education over the last four years as follows: "During her time as the coordinator, Mrs. Givens has experienced many successes. After doing such a great job in our elementary building she came to the middle and high school highly recommended and has lived up to that recommendation. She has tripled the numbers of the expanded learning programs during the school year and has fostered many relationships with staff, parents, community and the students.

Additionally, she has been responsible for coordinating and managing our growing summer program. She started four summers ago with approximately 120 students and has managed and coordinated programs for over 400 students at a time. Lastly, during her time of managing summer programs behavior issues have decreased."

LaKeitha is passionate about helping youth help themselves. She believes in offering emotional, academic and social support to all youth. Her motto is, "If a young person has a dream, then dream with them and help them obtain the tools they need in order to make the dream a reality."

LaKeitha has started a blog entitled, *#LaKeithasPerspective*. This is her way of empowering a community and giving hope. It is her desire to deal with the matters of the heart and help individuals get through the rough spots in life.

LaKeitha D. Givens

Facebook * LaKeithas Perspective

Facebook * LaKeitha Brooks-Givens

Email * Keithadoree1@yahoo.com

Blog * keithadoree1.wordpress.com

Know Your Mandate–
The Heart of a Faithful Father

One of the most needed gifts in the body of Christ is ironically also the most forsaken. The gift I speak of is the gift of spiritual fathers with the heart of a faithful father. The body is inundated with spiritual fathers in name, but few in heart. The 20th Century produced a multitude of Denominations, Organizations, Reformations, Fellowships and many other entities that allowed many in ministry to come into covenant connection supposedly for the sake of accountability and/or ministry support.

Of these entities, the leading figures are referred to as 'Spiritual Fathers or Spiritual Mothers.' To the dismay of many disillusioned followers, what was advertised and what was presented were not the same.

What was *supposed* to be a father or

mother, too often was nothing more
than egomaniacal eccentric or tyrannical
individuals, whose sole motivation was
(and is) power over the lives of other
people. In many cases the expected
worship of the leading figure exceeds
the worship of Jesus and anything
outside of absolute loyalty to the leader
was (and is) considered traitorous and
almost blasphemous.

The only people who are enhanced
(mostly financially) under this type of
regime are the leading figures
themselves, while the son or daughter is
more deficient in direction than when
they first connected.

I have found in most cases that the
aforementioned leaders lacked the aid
of spiritual parenting themselves and it
is difficult for them to be what they had
never been properly groomed to be. If
one does not have either a father or the
right father (mother where applicable),
it is difficult to be a father or the right
father. What remains is self-taught

leadership, without the benefit of checks and balances. When someone attempts to lead where they have never been, they misdirect others on their journeys.

True fathers were first true sons (daughters where applicable) and the knowledge and wisdom gained from that relationship gives proper preparation to become what your son-ship grooms you for and that is a father with the son's best interest in mind. This is because as a son, you have the father's best interest in mind and the seed of son-ship produces the harvest of fatherhood. The father is what the son was elevated to, with the same understanding that the essence of both levels is servitude.

The heart of a faithful father is filled with the understanding that to fulfill the mandate to get the son to the destination of their assignment requires serving the son, while the son is serving. Dr. Jonason Pack has an excellent book on son-ship entitled, *Sonship: The*

Strategy of Submission that positions sons in the selection pool from which fathers are taken. He brings out the essence of a son that should produce the strength and wisdom of a father.

If the son does not exceed the father in most areas of ministry, one of two things has happened: Either the father failed them or the son did not heed the wisdom of the father. It should be very difficult to exceed the wisdom of a father, because what you need in a father should increase as your need increases.

I sought that spiritual father for the greatest part of my ministry and because I have understood accountability and submission, I refused to be uncovered. This led to being submitted under the types of leaders that are described in the beginning and in some cases submitting to leaders that could not provide what I needed because they just didn't have it. This led to years of futility that I vowed to never be a leader that produced futility in another minister's life. When the Lord brought my true spiritual father into my life, I heard his voice before I saw his face and my spirit leapt in probably the same way that John leapt in Elizabeth's womb when she encountered a mutually pregnant Mary.

I knew immediately that this was the voice that I had been looking for my entire life and I did not hesitate to make it known. Apostle Lionel Childress, Sr. is the epitome of a spiritual father in that he has the combination of a powerful anointing, wisdom beyond comprehension, extremely gifted preacher and prophet, but also genuine humility and love unfeigned and the drive to see his spiritual children do the greater works. This is the type of father that I have always strived to be and it was only through the connection with this powerful man of God, that I could be even better at what I had always been pretty good at.

I will accept nothing less than my sons excelling in their own ministries as well as exceeding what I have done in ministry and life and the ability to insure that this is a reality is certainly more probable, now that my ability to do so has been enhanced by my access into the faithfulness of my father's heart. A true father relishes the success of his children rather than feel inferior by it. It in no way diminishes or demeans you as a father, when your children exceed your accomplishments or boundaries. To the contrary, it says volumes about the parent/child relationship, because the father was willing to guide and the child was willing to follow the guidance.

True fathers are always in search mode in order to discover and pioneer areas that the child is to go into, in order to lessen the difficulties when necessary. Some adverse experiences actually enhance the child to become more equipped to deal with the difficulties of life, more than the father trying to prevent every adverse experience. Sometimes the value of an experience is not realized until one has to pay for it, as opposed to every solution being given. The skill of the father is realized when the situation presents the opportunity to give the solution for it (if he has it), or to allow the child to find the solution based on lessons already learned.

The primary responsibilities of even biological fathers are to produce, train, guide and monitor their children's lives. One of the most misquoted and misused scriptures in the Bible is **Proverbs 13:22** that reads "A good man leaves an inheritance to his children's children: and the wealth of the sinner is laid up for the just." The church norm has been to present this solely as a financial mantra that has done more to create a covetous generation of waiting for what belongs to someone else, as opposed to looking at the deeper implications that reveal an understanding of moral responsibility. The amplified Bible version of the same scripture illustrates my point:

A good man leaves an inheritance [of moral stability and goodness] to his children's children, and the wealth of the sinner [finds its way eventually] into the hands of the righteous, for whom it was laid up.

This shows that first of all, the good man is a father with vision, because he is looking at the immediate father/son relationship with another generation in mind. The implication is that the son's children should benefit from the son's experiences, just as he is benefitting from his father's experiences. Note also, that the responsibility to teach moral responsibility, as well as giving wisdom and guidance comes before the mention of wealth, because fiscal responsibility without moral responsibility is a recipe for disaster. "For what profit a man to gain the whole world and lose his soul." **Matthew 16:26** The heart of a faithful father is filled with the desire to see his children in position to hear the words that all of God's people long to hear, and that is "Well done thy good and faithful servant."

~Dr. Leandrew 'Lee' Tyson

DR. *Leandrew 'Lee' Tyson* is the founder and Chief Apostle for *Kingdom Works Ministries, Inc.* (KWM), which was established in 1998 in Dallas, Texas. The vision of KWM was given to equip and empower leaders for 21st century ministry. The implementation of this vision has caused exponential growth worldwide and now encompasses over 80 churches, ministries and ministers nationally and abroad.

The leadership of Apostle Lee and Prophetess Joann (his wife of 14 years) serves as a model for the sons and daughters in the ministries that they cover. Their uncompromising emphasis on integrity, education and holy living, has caused ministries and ministers with a desire to be spiritually parented by ethical leaders, to seek them out and connect with the vision of KWM.

Apostle Lee was born in the west Texas town of Pecos to Leroy and Louise Tyson. He had his first encounter with the Lord at the age of 10 and preached his first sermon at the age of 12. He is a gifted preacher and teacher and his prophetic precision keeps his ministry in great demand. He is known for his wisdom and passion for souls and most of all, his love for God.

Dr. Leandrew 'Lee' Tyson

General Overseer-
Kingdom Works Global Ministries

Email * apostletyson@aol.com

Website * kwmglobalinc.com

Get In The Flow–
Prayer, Prophecy and Prosperity

"For prayer is what we are more than what we say". **–J. Robert Ashcroft.**

Prayer is one of the most intimate expressions of the bride of Christ life. Why, then, is it so neglected?

We live in a time that completely avoids intimacy and closeness. The disposition to avoid self-exposure and friendships, I believe, affects spiritual as well as interpersonal relationships. The body of Christ, without being fully aware that this spirit of the age has crept into the church, feel uncomfortable getting too close to God. Prayerlessness is the result and prayerlessness is really godlessness.

Prayer

I would like to name a few aspects of prayer. As each aspects of prayer is understood and applied to the life of the believer, a vital prayer life is not only possible to the church but to be expected.

1. <u>Adoration</u>. The word "adoration" is a form of respect, devotion and the demonstration of great love. Those who study the word of God know the word "adoration" is not in the bible (KJV or NIV), but words like "awe," "fear of the Lord," and worship." For the children of God, when we worship we are showing adoration.

2. <u>Communion</u>. I like the way one dictionary defines "communion" and that is "intimate fellowship." Look at **Exodus 25:22, II Corinthians13:14, I John 1:3, Philippians 2:1** for a deeper study. The word "communion" or

"fellowship" reveal unto me a merging of spirits into divine oneness, like unto the intertwining of cords into one rope.

3. <u>Intercession</u>. The verb form of the word intercession means literally 'to meet,' 'to put pressure on,' 'to encounter'; then 'to plead.' In the New Covenant, 'intercession' comes from the Greek word *entugchano*, which means 'to plead for,' 'to appeal to,' 'to pray,' 'to make intercession.' Look at **Romans 8:26, 27** and **I Timothy 2:1** for a deeper study. Understand that intercession is the act of a person or group of people human or divine, making entreaty to God in the place of another person or persons.

4. <u>Supplication</u>. One writer says "supplication is the act of making humble and earnest entreaty for favor, especially to God." The root word *hanan* in the Hebrew is translated 'supplication' or supplications.'

Sometimes it carries the idea of a strong request, intercession and petition. In some scriptures supplication or supplications is translated as 'beg for mercy,' 'prayer' and 'beg for favor.' Look at **I Kings 8:33, 34** and **Psalm 30:8** for a deeper study.

5. <u>Thanksgiving</u>. Thanksgiving is when the believers openly celebrates or acknowledge God's divine goodness. It can also mean a wide expression of gratitude toward the Father. In the Old Covenant the Hebrew verb *yadah* and noun *todah* are linked to thanks and thanksgiving. In other parts of scripture they are translated 'confession' and 'praise.' Look at **Psalm 69:30** for a deeper study. In the New Covenant, 'thanksgiving' proclaims praise and 'gratitude,' it means 'well' or 'good' and also (favor, thanks, graciousness, goodwill and grace). Look at **Philippians 4:6** for a deeper study. All during the day, the devout Jew praise

and thank God for all things with sentence prayers. Paul wrote in Thessalonians 'pray without ceasing.'

6. <u>Worship</u>. One writer says "worship is reverence extended to an esteemed supernatural being." I believe worship to a child of God is the lifestyle of expressing reverence, devotion and admiration to God Almighty. There are a large number of English words of worship translated 'bow down,' 'pay honor,' 'serve,' 'revere' and 'fear.' Look at **Psalm 29:2** for a deeper study. In the New Covenant the Greek word for 'worship' is *proskuneo* 'to fall down prostrate in reverence.' The word *proskunetes* means 'a worshiper.' Look at **John 4:23, 24** for a deeper study.

Prophecy

The next destiny flow to get in is Prophecy. Having a prophetic voice and activating your prophetic voice will yield you fruits of great joy while destiny is calling. I want to talk about three aspects of prophecy. I believe everyone reading this book is experiencing at least one of these aspects of prophecy in their life.

Three Aspects of Prophecy

1. <u>The Spirit of Prophecy</u>. "**5**After that thou shalt come to the hill of God, where is the garrison of the Philistines: and it shall come to pass, when thou art come thither to the city, that thou shalt meet a company of prophets coming down from the high place with a psaltery, and a tabret, and a pipe, and a harp, before them; and they shall prophesy: **6**And the Spirit of the Lord will come upon thee, and thou shalt prophesy with them, and shalt be turned into another man. **7**And let it be, when these signs are come unto thee,

that thou do as occasion serve thee; for God is with thee." **I Samuel 10:5-7**

The prophet Samuel is giving Saul a word of prophecy concerning how he will prophesy among the prophets. Saul is not a prophet, but *the spirit of prophecy* shall come upon him and Saul shall prophesy AMONG the company of prophets. *The spirit of prophecy* didn't fall on Saul until he was up under the prophetic umbrella of the company of prophets. The lesson I want you to learn when it comes to *the spirit of prophecy* is it is only activated when you are in the company of the prophet or if you are connected to a prophetic ministry and then the spirit of prophecy can and will come upon you without you ever being called to the office of the prophet.

2. <u>The Gift of Prophecy</u>. "For the gifts and calling of God are without repentance." **Romans 11:29**

I want to go deeper with this aspect of prophecy. When God gives a

person a gift, it's just that - a gift. For
those like myself who have the gift of
prophecy, it was given to me without
me repenting of my sins or going on a
40-day fast and consecration (which I
now do three times a year). There is
nothing of our doing that causes God to
give us *the gift of prophecy*.

I am about to go deeper - so stay
with me. Even the psychic can see in the
spirit realm although they may not be
using their gift for the glory of God. I
can remember times when I was a
young boy about 10 years of age and I
would have prophetic dreams. When I
would wake up I would tell my mother
what I dreamed and it would happen
the next day. Keep in mind I was not
saved. I had not accepted Jesus as my
Lord and savior. No one lead me
through the sinner's prayer. All I had
was the gift and the dreams happened
often. I would see angels in the spirit as
a young boy. Sometimes they would
reveal themselves in church, other times

I would be riding in the car with my mother or at the hospital visiting the saints of old.

The lesson I want you to learn when it comes to *the gift of prophecy* is that God decided to bless you with the gift. God did it without the vote of a board. He did it without even asking you if you wanted it!

3. <u>The Office of Prophecy</u>. "Having then gifts differing according to the grace that is given to us, whether prophecy, let us prophesy according to the proportion of faith;" **Romans 12:6**

The third aspect of prophecy is very extinctive and I will give you a general overview. For those of you who are reading this book and you know that you are called to the office of prophet, you may understand what I am about to say. However, for those who are learning about *the office of prophet* and you feel God is leading you into the office of the prophet this is for you.

Romans 12:6 gives a little more insight on aspect number two, *The Gift of Prophecy,* by telling the reader that having the gifts is according to the grace that is given to us. Every gift has attached to it a level of grace. What is grace? Grace is God's unmerited favor. Grace is getting something that you don't deserve, but because of Grace God tells you, "Access granted."

Then the Apostle Paul goes further and says something that shifted my prophetic anointing to a new dimension. He said, "Let us prophesy according to the proportion of faith." My eyes were opened and I came into a spiritual awakening. You create prophesy with your faith.

The Office of Prophecy carries with it a key called faith that is the master key in every realm. Let's go deeper, the prophet that walks in the *Office of Prophecy* at times will not hear God say anything about a situation because God is waiting on that prophet to prophesy

according to the proportion or measure
of their faith.

    There will be times that God will
not show the prophet anything because
God wants the prophet to prophesy the
victory according to the measure of their
faith.

    The lesson I want you to learn
when it comes to *The Office of Prophecy* is
that God has given you the authority as
a prophet to call those things that are
not as though they are.

Prosperity

    My assignment to the body of
Christ in this season is to share life-
changing spiritual principles about
success and prosperity found in the
Word of God to help you rid yourself of
the self-defeating mindset of negativity
and doubt, replacing it with power-
packed words of wisdom from God that

will bring the fruit of joy and abundance in your life.

As an Apostle I assure you that it is right and good that you should have success and good fortune, for the Lord wants you to live victoriously in every area of your life.

Prosperity is a Divine Heritage for God's people. It is your right to have God's prosperity, but you must believe it before it will manifest in your life. Prosperity is more than just money. Prosperity is abundant living in every area of your life *Spiritual, Physical, Mental, Emotional and Financial.*

God has a flow for all the days of your life that involves goodness and mercy. "Surely goodness and mercy shall follow me all the days of my life: and I will dwell in the house of the Lord forever." **Psalm 23:6**

Whenever you open your mouth and shout for joy and declare that the Lord be magnified, God finds pleasure in prospering you. "Let them shout for joy and be glad, that favour my righteous cause: yea, let them say continually, Let the Lord be magnified, which hath pleasure in the prosperity of his servant." **Psalm 35:27**

Let the Redeemed Say So

We are constantly reminded throughout the Bible that the words of our mouth play an important part in the creation of our desired success, health and wealth. In **Psalms**, David appeals to the Lord that his words will be found good and acceptable, "Let the words of my mouth and the meditation of my heart, be acceptable in thy sight, O Lord, my strength and my redeemer." **Psalm 19:14** Disciplining your mind to think on good things and then to speak them will bring forth rich results for you and those around you. You need to 'speak' what you desire. "Let the redeemed of the Lord say so, whom he hath redeemed from the hand of the enemy;" **Psalm 107:2**

Prosperity Activation

Declare the following powerful prosperity activations out loud with great emotion and feeling and watch as more prosperity begin to flow into your life in an abundant way. I know for a fact that this spiritual principle will cause your prosperity to be activated in every area of your life.

I love the highest and best in me. I now draw the highest and best people to me.

Everything and everybody prospers me now. I prosper everything and everybody.

God's rich good now comes rushing into my life health, wealth, success and great prosperity. All those good things and more are attracted to me.

Every day in every way I am growing richer and richer. Success is being multiplied in my life. Money, health, riches and prosperity come to me now. Wealth rushes out to meet me. Yes, it meets me more than half way. Praise the Lord.

Speak Words of Plenty ~ Not Lack

It is always unwise to magnify financial difficulties. In difficult financial periods, it is better to re-affirm words of success. You should say things like: "I have faith that this shall pass." Then start building and holding to high financial visions of success and prosperity. Welcome with open arms the idea of money, success, plenty and prosperity to your door steps.

All financial doors are open. All financial channels are free. Endless bounty of good now flows in my life. It now comes to me. It rushes towards me and meets me more than half way.

God is in charge of my life. Only His rich good now appears in my life. Health, wealth and riches adore me and now come rushing into my home.

God is in charge of my life. I am now open, receptive and obedient to His rich instructions and guidance.

If you put these prosperity activations to work in your life every day for 30 days when you wake up in the morning and just before going to bed and repeat them over and over again until they get down in your spirit you will be in the flow of great prosperity.

Can you hear it? Destiny is calling. Get in the flow!

~Apostle C.D. Dixon

APOSTLE *Chester Damond Dixon* received the call to the gospel ministry at the age of sixteen and began moving in the things of God immediately! Having exemplified strong leadership qualities at an early age, he became a role model for his peers and excelled in his academic studies.

The Lord birthed a powerful ministry out of Apostle Dixon's spirit called *C.D. Dixon Ministries*. He attended Prairie View University, majoring in General Business. Apostle Dixon also attended Southwestern Assemblies of God University (SAGU), where his area of concentration was Pastoral Ministry.

While attending SAGU, Apostle Dixon was also Co-Pastor of *God's Love Prayer House Ministries* in Dallas, Texas founded and Pastored by his mother Beverly J. Baylock-Dixon.

Apostle Dixon is united in holy matrimony with his lovely wife Prophetess Nell Dixon and they have three beautiful children Demarius, Taylor and Chesteria.

Apostle C.D. Dixon formerly Pastored *Houston Spiritual Temple World Headquarters.* In 1996 the Lord anointed Apostle Dixon as an Apostle. God always anoint before He appoints. Now Apostle Dixon is walking in the appointment of his apostolic calling.

In January 2009 *Woodland Spiritual Temple,* the second Spiritual Temple was erected by the 'Hand of God' through the 'Vessel of God!'

Apostle Dixon is the Prophetic Overseer of many conferences and events such as:

40 Days of Fasting & Praying,
Couples with a Love Affair,
Empowering the Business Mind,
Supernatural Encounter,
Prophetic Youth Explosion,

He has conducted revivals, crusades and conferences in various cities and states. Apostle Dixon has also appeared on several radio stations, internet radio and television programs. God commissioned Apostle Dixon to write a book entitled *An In-depth Study of Prayer*.

Apostle Dixon is the CEO and Founder of a powerful prayer ministry called *Spiritual Kingdom Gate Keepers* (SKGK). God has allowed this broken vessel to minister to countless people who have been set free by the power of God's anointing flowing heavily through his preaching and teaching.

With the fivefold ministry at work in his life and having a heavy apostolic and prophetic mantle, Apostle C.D. Dixon has a contemporary ministry on the 'cutting edge' of the millennium. His visionary mandate is to stir up ministry gifts in the body of Christ, equipping men and women for the Kingdom of God and spiritual warfare. Thus, bringing them to a depth of knowledge, revelation and maturity in the things of God so as to effectuate the culmination of the unfinished task of preparing a bride adorned for her husband.

Apostle C. D. Dixon

C.D. Dixon Ministries
820 S. MacArthur Blvd. Suite 105-166
Coppell, Texas 75019

Phone * 972-510-5574

You Tube* ApostleCDDixon

Facebook * CDDixonministries

Twitter * ApostleCDDixon

Instagram * ApostleCDDixon

Email *
CD_DixonMinistries@yahoo.com

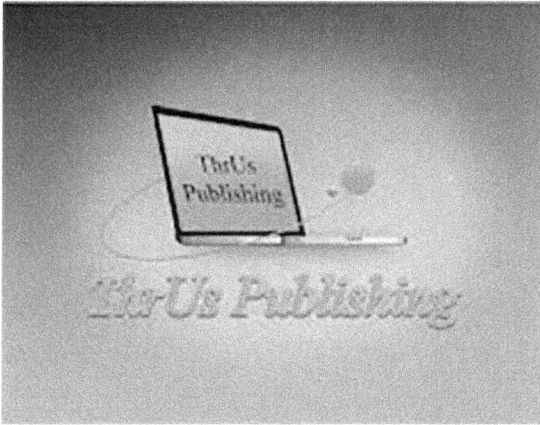

"Birthing Books. Changing Lives."

WWW.THRUSPUBLISHING.COM

www.ingramcontent.com/pod-product-compliance
Lightning Source LLC
Chambersburg PA
CBHW072002040426
42447CB00009B/1445